"DRIVE illustrates the five buying personalities. The good news is you already speak one. The bad news is you're accidentally alienating the other four which is costing you sales. Learn the missing four buying personalities and you have the potential to increase your sales by 400%."

Garrett Gunderson
New York Times Bestselling Author of Killing Sacred Cows

"After I trained with Woody I cleared six figures on my first keynote speech by implementing DRIVE. This system will forever change your sales."

Ron Williams
7-time Mr. Natural Olympia
7-time Mr. Natural Universe
7-time Mr. Natural World

"At JetBlue I taught my team how to use DRIVE to resolve customer concerns, lower employee turnover, and increase team morale. DRIVE is my go-to system to increase customer engagement."

Anna Smith
JetBlue Senior CSVC

"I invited Woody to speak at one of my international events. I challenged him to use DRIVE to sell one of MY products, not his. When the final numbers came in, he increased my sales by 1440%. If you want to change your sales numbers read this book."

Rob Sperry
The Game of Networking

"The DRIVE Sales System has helped us raise $2,386,400 in capital for investments. When you are negotiating terms, knowing the DRIVE of the person sitting across the table from you is a game-changer."

Daniel and Sam Kwak
Investors

"Since being introduced to DRIVE my philosophy of business management and entrepreneurship has changed significantly. DRIVE centered strategies and business plans produce results! It takes the 'guessing' out of sales, marketing, and managing staff."

Matthew Casto
Senior Art Director, Universal Studios

"In three years, I took my company from my garage to being one of Inc 500's Fastest Growing Companies. Woody has been my business strategist for over 10 years, and I attribute so much of my success, both personally and financially, to his brilliant DRIVE program."

Inger Erickson
Uppercase Living

"I had the honor of having Woody perform the true power of DRIVE in front of a live audience at an event I ran in Australia. It was so powerful the audience demanded additional training. We had to change the agenda to make room for him to dive deeper. It was one of the most relevant and mind-blowing trainings I have ever witnessed."

Frazer Brookes
Social Media Strategist

"If you are a mind reader, you do NOT need this book. But if by chance you find yourself lacking in mind-reading skills—activate the DRIVE Sales System immediately. It will give you laser focus on closing more sales and increasing your income."

Troy Dunn
TV Host

"DRIVE not only increased my business and our non-profit, it has enlightened us to know how to empower others! DRIVE took us to the next level!"

Leesa Price
CEO Princess Warrior

"IT WORKS! We have grown our business by almost 100% since implementing the DRIVE Sales System."

Eric Counts
Founder of CreditNerds.com

"When I first met Woody I was already successful but lost in my own world. Through his DRIVE system I learned how to create myself as an asset and how to start attracting all the right people and situations into my life. With his help my life took off and I've been able to create a life I never dreamed of before. This book is a must-read, more so for one's self but also for their business."

Jimmy Rex
You End Up Where You're Heading

"DRIVE has taken my sales to the next level by helping me understand how to identify the five buying personality types. If you are looking to increase your sales and gain a new mindset, skillset, and toolset—this book delivers."

Cody Hofhine
Co-Founder Wholesaling Inc.

"Woody is one of the most creative people I've ever met. He has the ability to break complex subjects into simple, step by step concepts. This is what he has done with sales in DRIVE. If you want to sell more, and if you want to know why your prospects are buying from you, then you need DRIVE."

Justin Prince
Be the One

"You cannot make a difference in the lives of others until you know what DRIVEs them. Being able to connect on a deep intimate level will allow you to create wealth in your life, relationships, and in your business."

Greg S. Reid
Think and Grow Rich; Three Feet from Gold

"DRIVE is a wonderful tool I highly recommend for you to discover who you really are, which will allow you to have more love, wealth, health, and joy in your life."

Jack Canfield
New York Times Bestselling Co-Author of Chicken Soup for the Soul

"As you begin to understand your DRIVE and gain insight into yourself, it gives you a greater insight into others, and insight allows you to make a greater impact in life."

Les Brown
Laws of Success

"When you are marketing to someone, you must understand their DRIVE to trigger their buying buttons. Woody Woodward will teach you how to discover your customer's DRIVE and what causes them to buy more."

Joel Comm
New York Times Bestselling Author of Twitter Power

D.R.I.V.E.
SALES SYSTEM

D.R.I.V.E.

SALES SYSTEM

The 5 Steps to Increasing Your Sales Reach by 400%

Bob Snyder and Woody Woodward

RENEGADE
PUBLISHING

Warning—Disclaimer

The purpose of this book is to educate and inspire. It is not intended to give advice, make promises, or guarantees that anyone following the ideas, tips, suggestions, techniques, or strategies will have the same results as the people listed throughout the stories contained herein. The author, publisher, and distributor(s) shall have neither liability nor responsibility to anyone with respect to any loss or damage caused, or alleged to be caused, directly or indirectly, by the information. The author has used interviews, biographies, and documentaries to give the best educated guess on all the individuals' DRIVE referenced in this book. No guarantees are implied or granted.

ISBN 978-1-7353317-7-5
Printed in the United States of America

Dedication

To all our incredible clients, This book is a testament to the thousands of conversations we've shared about DRIVE. Your unwavering commitment to building your business and transforming relationships has been the driving force behind these pages. Without your passion, insights, and dedication, this work would not exist. May you take pride in knowing that your journey and discoveries are woven into every chapter. This is for you.

Bob:

To Holly, the love of my life, you ground me and inspire me to be the best I can be. Your patience and sacrifice over the last 4 decades are a testament to your character, your love, and your compassion for this flawed man. Thank you. And to Woody, DRIVE's creator genius, thank you for allowing me to be a part of this great work. DRIVE is the ultimate force multiplier and the world of sales and business will forever be changed because of you.

Woody:

To my dearest wife and children, you have sacrificed the most, and no worldly accolade or success could ever truly repay the depth of that sacrifice. Your unwavering support and love are the foundation of everything I do. Without you, none of this would exist. And to Bob, who gave me the greatest advice ever: "Don't Be Stupid! You are not done developing DRIVE. Keep going." Without his encouragement and wise counsel this work would not be what it is today. I will be forever grateful for your visionary counsel. You are the difference maker.

Contents

"100% of Customers are People.
100% of Employees are People.
If You Don't Understand People,
You Don't Understand Business."
—Simon Sinek

—◦◦◦—

Sales is the Solution

What would happen if, in the next twenty-four hours, every sales-person on the planet disappeared? There would be no more pesky sales calls. No more obnoxious marketing. There also wouldn't be anyone pitching new ideas. No one selling innovative tools, equipment, medicine, or food.

What would happen next? Within a week, the economy would crumble. Factory assembly lines grind to a halt because no one is buying their supplies. Hospital shelves go bare without anyone selling them life-saving medicine. Farmers stop planting; without contracts, there are no crops and no food. Innovation dies since no one is selling investors on the next big thing.

And within a month? Civilization collapses. **The world burns. The end.**

Sound extreme? It's not. Every great invention, breakthrough, and movement in history started with a sale. After all, the Founding Fathers had to sell their revolution. The Wright brothers had to sell flight itself. Henry Ford had to sell the world on cars. Steve Jobs had to sell the novel idea of personal computers and smartphones. Without sales, nothing happens.

The Manipulation Myth

People don't hate sales. They hate bad salespeople. They've been burned before—by the pushy car salesman, the telemarketer who won't take no for an answer, or the scammer selling dreams that never materialize. But here's the truth: bad salespeople aren't salespeople. They're con artists.

A con artist lies to win. A great salesperson wins by telling the truth.

A con artist gets the sale by deception. A great salesperson gets the sale by making someone's life better.

A con artist traps people into a deal they regret. A great salesperson guides people to a decision they thank them for.

People think sales is about convincing, persuading, using sales rebuttals, or even manipulation. However, the best salespeople don't push. They inspire action. They don't force people to buy—they help people make the best possible decision for their future. They don't "close deals." They open opportunities. They don't pressure. They guide.

Why Sales is the Most Honest Profession on Earth

In most jobs, people get paid whether they perform positively or not for their client. A lawyer gets his or her retainer whether they win or lose their case. A doctor gets paid whether the patient gets better or not. A corporate executive receives their check even if the company tanks.

But sales? If you lie, manipulate, or sell garbage, you will be exposed. If you aren't authentic and don't excel at what you do, you will not make a dime. Sales isn't a game of manipulation; it's a game of value.

The best salespeople win because they help people improve their lives—not by tricking them into something they don't need.

What's the world's oldest profession? Ask most people, and they'll smirk and say prostitution. It's been repeated so often, it's practically gospel.

But it's wrong.

The oldest recorded transactions weren't about sex. They were about trade. Cuneiform tablets from Mesopotamia, dated back to 3000 BC, show something revolutionary: the first documented open markets. The Sumerians were exchanging goods, negotiating prices, and striking deals. But sales didn't start with the Sumerians. It started the moment human beings first communicated.

If you believe in the biblical origin of humanity, then the first transaction wasn't silver or livestock—it was persuasion. But not all persuasion is equal. Satan wasn't selling; he was conning. His pitch? "Eat this, and you'll be like God." He sold Eve on a false promise, a sleazy deception wrapped in the illusion of value, coming from a skilled con artist.

But Eve? She was the first real salesperson. Adam had everything—paradise, abundance, even divine favor. But Eve had to sell him on what he lacked: partnership, shared experience, and a future beyond solitude. If he didn't partake, he'd remain alone in a perfect world, missing the one thing that made it meaningful. Her sale wasn't built on deception. It was built on vision, connection, and the truth that life is only fully lived when it's shared.

If you lean toward an evolutionary viewpoint, imagine the earliest humans struggling to survive in an unforgiving world. Isolation meant death—strength came from the tribe. Those who conned, stole, or manipulated were cast out, left to fend for themselves against fierce predators and the harsh elements. Only those who created value—those who had something to offer—were welcomed, protected, and given a place in the group.

Now, picture two early humans: one has mastered fire, the other has perfected the spear. Neither can thrive alone, but together? They

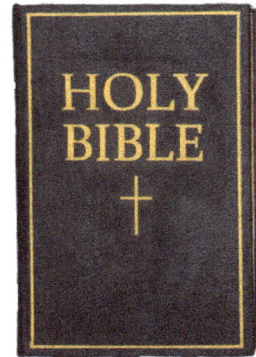

can shape the future. "I'll teach you fire if you give me a spear." That moment when one created value for the other, trading not just goods but survival itself, was the first sale in human history.

And just like that, sales became the foundation of civilization. Not manipulation, and not deception, but value. The ones who provided it weren't just accepted. They were vital.

Before money, before contracts, and before economies, there was only one thing that made sales possible: trust. The first merchants had to prove to people their goods were worth trading for. The first deals were made on a handshake, a promise, or a belief. The first salespeople weren't selling products; they were selling possibilities.

Sales is not a modern invention. And at the core of every sale—whether it was Sumerian merchants, cavemen, or Apple selling iPhones—there has always been one reason people buy: personal improvement.

The Universal Law of Sales

Nobody buys a product.
Nobody buys a service.
Nobody buys a strategy.

They buy a better version of themselves.

No one buys a car. They buy freedom, status, or reliability. No one buys a phone. They buy connection, productivity, and entertainment. No one buys weight loss programs. They buy confidence and energy. No one buys an expensive watch. They buy significance and recognition. No one buys a business strategy. They buy profit and security.

People don't spend money unless it improves their life, relationships, or career.

Most salespeople focus on the product. That's a mistake. Great salespeople focus on the transformation.

You're not selling a fitness program. You're selling energy, confidence, and a better body.

You're not selling a remote work solution. You're selling freedom and control over your time.

You're not selling software. You're selling efficiency and saved hours.

You're not selling a service. You're selling peace of mind.

When you understand this, you stop selling and start serving. The best salespeople don't make people want something. They show people why they can't live without it.

Blockbuster's $50 Million Blunder

In the early 2000s, Blockbuster was an unstoppable giant. With over 9,000 stores worldwide and 65 million registered customers, it dominated the home entertainment industry. Movie nights meant driving to Blockbuster, wandering the aisles with your family, hoping your movie was in stock, and collecting your favorite snacks at checkout.

And if you returned the VHS or DVD late? You got slapped with a late fee—a business model that made them billions but angered customers.

Then came Netflix.

At the time, Netflix was a scrappy DVD-by-mail service, bleeding cash and struggling to survive. In 2000, co-founders Reed Hastings and Marc Randolph flew to Dallas and sat across the table from Blockbuster's CEO, John Antioco. Their offer? "Buy Netflix for $50 million, and we'll run your online division."

Antioco and his team laughed them out of the room. Who would ever wait for a DVD in the mail when they could just drive to a store and get one instantly? That moment—that arrogance—sealed Blockbuster's fate.

Netflix wasn't selling DVDs. They were selling convenience. They eliminated late fees, introduced a subscription model, and focused on giving customers what they actually wanted—the ultimate improvement—unlimited movies without getting in the car. It just took a quick walk to their mailbox.

Blockbuster doubled down on their stores, convinced their dominance would last. Netflix's next step was betting everything on streaming. No more physical DVDs, no more waiting—just instant entertainment. By the time Blockbuster finally tried to catch up, launching a DVD-by-mail service and eventually dipping into streaming, Netflix had already won.

Blockbuster came to the realization that their customers no longer wanted to drive to a store, yet Netflix had already given them a better way.

In 2010, Blockbuster filed for bankruptcy.

Netflix? It's now worth over $423 billion.

Takeaway: Blockbuster thought they were in the movie rental business. Netflix knew they were in the business of delivering entertainment with zero friction. One focused on selling a product. The other sold a better experience.

Kodak: The Billion-Dollar Blind Spot

In 1975, inside the research labs of Kodak, a young engineer named Steve Sasson created something that should have changed the world: the first digital camera. It was a crude device by today's standards, a shoebox-sized contraption that took black-and-white images and stored them on a cassette tape. But it worked.

Excited about the breakthrough, Sasson presented it to Kodak's executives, expecting a mix of shock and enthusiasm. Instead, he was met with blank stares and a cold response.

"That's cute," one executive said. "But don't tell anyone about it."

Kodak was the undisputed king of photography. But they didn't just sell the cameras themselves; they sold film. Their entire business model relied on customers buying roll after roll of film to capture their memories. A camera that didn't need film? That wasn't an opportunity—it was a threat.

So, they buried it.

For nearly three decades, Kodak ignored the shift happening in front of them. They had the technology, the patents, and the resources to dominate the future of photography. But instead of selling customers a better way to capture memories, they kept trying to sell them what had worked in the past.

Meanwhile, digital photography advanced. Companies like Sony and Canon capitalized on what a Kodak engineer had created but refused to embrace. Then came the smartphone revolution. Suddenly, people didn't need film—or even a camera—because the ability to take, store, and share photos was in their pocket.

By the time Kodak finally started pushing into digital, it was too late. Their competitors had already taken the lead. The customers who once swore by Kodak had moved on, not because they wanted to, but because someone else offered them something better.

Then came the final nail in the coffin.

In 2012, Kodak filed for bankruptcy. That same year, a tiny app with no cameras, no film, and no legacy in photography—Instagram—sold for $1 billion.

The irony? More photos are taken today than at any other point in history. The demand for capturing memories didn't go away—it exploded. Kodak's failure wasn't a lack of innovation. It was a failure to sell people the improvement they wanted.

Takeaway: Customers don't buy products—they buy progress. And if you're too busy protecting what used to work, someone else will sell them a smarter, faster, and more valuable way forward.

Barnes & Noble's $2.4 Trillion Mistake

Barnes & Noble was once untouchable. It was the largest bookseller in America, with superstores in every major city and a loyal customer base that made it the undisputed king of the book industry. Amazon, by contrast, was a tiny online bookstore with no physical locations, no major distribution network, and no real power. It was barely a blip on Barnes & Noble's radar.

But Barnes & Noble forgot why people buy books. Typically, it isn't merely for the sake of owning paper and ink. They buy books for entertainment, knowledge, and self-improvement. And Amazon wasn't around to just sell books—it was selling a better way to get what people actually wanted.

In 1996, Barnes & Noble's chairman, Len Riggio, and his brother Stephen flew to Seattle to meet Jeff Bezos over dinner. They made their position clear: "We're launching our own online bookstore, and we're going to crush you." At the same time, they floated the idea of a partnership, maybe even licensing Amazon's technology. Bezos and his team politely declined. Amazon wasn't looking to join forces. It was looking to dominate.

Barnes & Noble quickly launched Barnesandnoble.com in 1997, but they made a critical mistake: they treated their website as a side project instead of a central revolution. Meanwhile, Amazon focused entirely on making book-buying cheaper, faster, and easier. Customers didn't need to leave their house. They didn't have to search for a title in a store. With one click, their book was on its way.

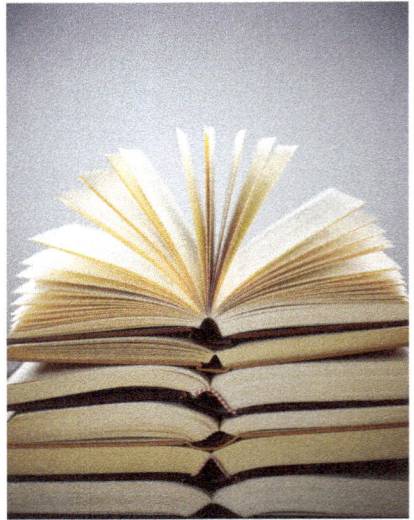

Then came Kindle. In 2007, Amazon introduced an e-reader that put an entire library in people's hands. Barnes & Noble dismissed the invention. "People will always prefer physical books," their leadership claimed. Two years later, when they finally launched the Nook, Amazon had already built an entire digital ecosystem—Kindle Direct Publishing, Audible, and exclusive deals with authors. The Nook? It was too little, too late.

By the time Barnes & Noble recognized that the future of books wasn't in physical stores, Amazon had already redefined the market. In 2019, Barnes & Noble was sold for approximately $683 million, a stark contrast to Amazon's market cap of $2.4 trillion. This disparity underscores a fundamental truth: while Barnes & Noble focused on just selling products, Amazon focused on delivering the improvements customers sought—convenience, accessibility, and a seamless reading experience. By prioritizing customer-centric innovation, Amazon transformed how the world reads.

Takeaway: Barnes & Noble sold books. Amazon sold convenience, speed, and an experience that redefined what buying could be. People don't reward tradition. They reward transformation.

The Cheat Code to Sales Mastery

If you've made it this far, we can agree upon one undeniable truth: sales is the engine of human progress. Without sales, the world stops.

But here's where most salespeople fail. They don't sell the improvement itself.

They push products instead of transformation. They pitch features instead of freedom, security, confidence, or time saved. They lose deals, not because their product isn't good, but because they spoke the wrong language.

Here's the reality: people don't buy for the same personal improvement.

Some crave freedom—the ability to make their own choices and forge their own path.

Some value relationships—they want to feel connected, trusted, and supported.

Some need logic and data—they won't buy unless it makes absolute sense.

Some seek recognition and validation—they need to know they're making the right decision.

Some are driven by results—they don't care about the process, just the outcome.

Every person buys based on one of these five core motivations. That's why the DRIVE Sales System is your cheat code.

It doesn't just teach you how to sell. It teaches you how to speak the five distinct buying languages that drive every person's decision. It's the difference between guessing what someone wants and knowing exactly how to position your offer so they can't say no.

This is how the world's greatest salespeople win consistently. They sell the exact improvement their buyer craves. And now, so can you.

Welcome to the DRIVE Sales System. The game is about to change.

2

Missed Opportunities

This is madness. No one's going to drive twenty-five miles to the middle of nowhere just to visit this place. He's lost it. After everything he's built, this is how he goes broke?

These thoughts must have raced through Arthur's mind as he stepped out of Walter's car, the dry California heat settling over them like a weight. They had driven far beyond the city, their tires kicking up dust on an empty road that felt like it led to nowhere. The late afternoon sun stretched shadows across a landscape of weeds and silence, broken only by the rustling of the wind through the orange groves. The place was a void—flat, unremarkable, and forgettable.

But Walter didn't see empty space. He saw a world waiting to be built.

He stepped onto the dirt road, his eyes burning with excitement, his vision already decades ahead of reality. "Art, this is it."

Arthur leaned against the car, arms crossed, his expression a mix of amusement and skepticism. He glanced around at the barren landscape. In his opinion, there was nothing here but a whole lot of wishful thinking.

"I can handle the main project myself," Walter told him. "It'll take everything I have, but I want you to have the first chance at buying the surrounding acreage. In the next five years, its value will skyrocket."

Arthur hesitated. He admired Walter's ambition, but this wasn't just a gamble—it was a long shot. He searched for the right words, not wanting to crush his friend's dream. Walter kept pressing, urging him to see the opportunity right in front of him, but Arthur wouldn't budge. He offered polite excuses—money was tight, and the timing wasn't right.

Trying to be encouraging, he added, "Maybe later."

Walter shook his head. "Later will be too late," he warned. "You need to move on this now."

But Arthur never moved.

One year later, on July 17, 1955, Walt Disney opened Disneyland—and Art Linkletter, his longtime friend, was the Master of Ceremonies on opening day.

As Art stood on stage, microphone in hand, watching thousands of families flood through the gates, reality must have hit him like a freight train. He wasn't just hosting an opening ceremony—he was watching his missed opportunity play out in real time. He had passed on the investment of a lifetime.

But while Linkletter didn't see the vision, someone else did.

That same year, while Disneyland was still under construction, the Fujishige family quietly purchased fifty-six acres of strawberry fields across the street for $3,500.

Decades later, in the late 1990s, Disney paid the family nearly $100 million for the land Linkletter had refused.

So, whose fault was it that Linkletter missed out? Was it Disney's, or was it Linkletter's?

Based on what we established in Chapter 1—that the whole purpose of sales is to serve, and that the only reason someone buys is for improvement—it was Walt's fault. He didn't create enough value for Linkletter to see how purchasing the land would benefit him.

The 20/80 Rule:
Why Do Salespeople Lose 80% of Their Sales
the Moment They Open Their Mouth?

Every salesperson has had that moment.

You walked out of a meeting, convinced you nailed it. The prospect nodded along, smiled, laughed at all your jokes, and even threw in a comment like, "This is really interesting." You left thinking, *Done deal. Easy money.*

Then? Crickets.

Days pass. Even weeks. You follow up. Nothing. You got ghosted harder than a bad Tinder date. What happened?

You delivered a perfect pitch if you were speaking to *yourself.* The excitement and passion you showcased in that meeting would have worked flawlessly on someone who thought and felt the same way you do. But guess what? Your prospective client only speaks the same "buying language" as you twenty percent of the time.

This is the **20/80 Rule** in action.

You Lose 80% of Sales
Because You Sell From Your Own D.R.I.V.E.,
Alienating the Other Four.

Most salespeople sell the way they want to buy. They assume their prospects value the same things they do, think the same way, and are motivated by the same factors. They're wrong.

Your DRIVE only represents 20% of buyers—which means that 80% of your audience tunes out the moment you start talking.

Why DRIVE Changes Everything

Based on the DRIVE framework, Walt Disney was a Director—a visionary who lived for big, bold ideas. When he tried to sell the idea of Disneyland to Art Linkletter, he pitched it like a Director: "Look at the innovation! The adventure! This groundbreaking idea will change the world!"

But Linkletter wasn't a Director. He was a Validator.

He wasn't motivated by risk, creativity, or thrill—he was motivated by admiration, status, and social influence. Buying the acreage next to Disneyland didn't validate him. It didn't elevate his standing, expand his influence, or cement his legacy. So he passed on the opportunity.

Meanwhile, the Fujishige family—Executives—bought the land immediately. They weren't interested in vision or status. They saw hard numbers, investment potential, and long-term gains.

Have you ever walked into a store excited to buy something—a new car, a sleek gadget, or the perfect living room set—only to have the salesperson kill your enthusiasm within minutes? They launch into their pitch, rattling off features and benefits, completely missing what actually matters to you. Instead of drawing you in, they push you away.

By the time they're done talking, your interest is gone. Sometimes, the pitch is so bad you don't just walk away—you make a mental note never to come back.

For over a century, sales books have promised "the secret to influence." Yet, despite all the techniques, strategies, and scripts, the average closing ratio has barely budged from that 20%. According to three independent studies from Harvard Business Review, Salesforce, and

HubSpot, salespeople convert just one in five prospects—leaving millions of missed deals and untapped revenue on the table.

Why? Because they aren't speaking their client's DRIVE.

History's Biggest Missed Sales

Not convinced?

Let's talk about some of the worst sales mistakes in history. These aren't bad ideas or even bad products. They are real-world examples of what happens when people aren't speaking the right buying language.

- Alexander Graham Bell offered Western Union the telephone for $100,000. They passed.

- Decca Records rejected The Beatles, saying "Guitar groups are on the way out."

- MySpace could have bought Facebook for $75 million. They passed.

- Excite could have bought Google for $750,000 in 1999. Two years later, Excite filed for bankruptcy.

- The founders of Airbnb offered 10% of their company to seven different VC firms for $150,000. They all passed.

- Steve Jobs offered his first boss, Nolan Bushnell, one-third of Apple for $50,000. Bushnell declined. Today, that would be worth $1.2 trillion.

- Billionaire Ross Perot could have owned a majority of Microsoft in 1979 for $60 million. That stake would now be worth $1.5 trillion.

Let's be clear: traditionally, your product isn't the problem. Neither is your price. It's not even your pitch—it's *whose* pitch you're giving. You're selling the way you want to buy instead of the way your prospective client needs to hear it. That's the real problem. The good news? There's a way to fix it.

The DRIVE Sales System: How to Sell to Every Buying Personality

Your prospects don't care about what excites you—they care about what excites them. And what excites them depends entirely on their DRIVE.

There are five buying personalities, and each one has specific motivations that influence their decisions. If you want to stop losing 80% of your sales, you need to sell in their language.

Understanding DRIVE is like unlocking a cheat code for influence. The moment you speak your prospect's buying language, resistance doesn't just crumble—it disappears. They don't need to be convinced, pressured, or "closed." They see it. They feel it. Now, they can't imagine life without it.

Your product isn't just something they're considering—it's something that feels inevitable. A perfect fit. A no-brainer. The missing piece they didn't even realize was missing until now.

Each person has a Primary DRIVE—the emotional reason they buy—and a Secondary DRIVE—the logical reason they say yes. These five DRIVEs are universal, and once you know them, you'll never see people the same way again.

Let's break them down, starting with the one that values freedom above all else.

Director (D)

Directors are risk-takers, pioneers, and independent thinkers. They don't buy products—they buy freedom.

- **Freedom & Autonomy**—Prefers products that offer independence and control.
- **Innovation & Creativity**—Drawn to unique, groundbreaking solutions.
- **Challenge & Adventure**—Seeks experiences that push boundaries.

How to Sell to a Director

Give them options, not restrictions. Highlight how your product gives them freedom, makes them feel like a trailblazer, or allows them to experience life on their terms.

Relator (R)

Relators buy based on emotion, relationships, and community. They don't care about cutting-edge tech or prestige—they care about people.

- **Relationship & Community**—Values products that strengthen connections.
- **Personal Influence**—Attracted to items that help them inspire others.
- **Service & Care**—Prefers solutions that enhance caregiving and support.

How to Sell to a Relator:

Make it personal. Show them how your product will improve their relationships, enhance their influence, or allow them to serve and support their loved ones.

Intellectual (I)

Intellectuals are logic-driven, analytical, and always seeking knowledge. They don't buy based on hype—they buy based on proof.

- **Knowledge & Learning**—Seeks products that expand understanding.
- **Organization & Efficiency**—Values tools that streamline tasks.
- **Health & Nature**—Drawn to wellness and environmentally connected products.

How to Sell to an Intellectual

Speak with logic and depth. Provide well-researched insights, emphasize organization and efficiency, and connect to their pursuit of knowledge, health, or higher standards.

Validator (V)

Validators are status-driven, recognition-seeking, and prestige-oriented. They don't just buy products—they buy identity.

- **Recognition & Status**—Prefers brands that enhance prestige.
- **Trust & Reliability**—Values proven quality and credibility.
- **Acceptance & Belonging**—Drawn to exclusivity and social validation.

How to Sell to a Validator

Give them respect and recognition. Show how your product elevates their status, builds trust, and reinforces their strengths in a way that makes them feel personally valued.

Executive (E)

Executives are goal-oriented, competitive, and results-driven. They don't buy dreams—they buy success.

- **Winning & Achievement**—Seeks tools for success and competition.
- **Control & Influence**—Prefers solutions that enhance authority.
- **Goal-Orientation**—Drawn to products that ensure results and security.

How to Sell to an Executive

Focus on results. Demonstrate how your product helps them win, stay in control, and achieve measurable success with security and efficiency.

The DRIVE Audition

Will you come to Australia's Gold Coast and share DRIVE with some of the top leaders in direct selling?

Rob Sperry, one of the most respected sales trainers in the industry, had just sent me a text inviting me to speak at an event he and Frazer Brookes were hosting. But this wasn't just a speaking gig—it was an audition.

What I didn't know at the time was that Frazer was watching me closely. If I could deliver enough value, he'd bring me to the UK to train 2,000 of the world's top direct salespeople. If I didn't? I'd never step on that stage. It was an all-or-nothing moment—one every salesperson understands.

The first day, I presented DRIVE, and the response was electric. They asked me to speak again the next day. This time, I only had thirty minutes and I knew this was my shot.

During the first fifteen minutes, I broke down how people buy based on their DRIVE. But then a thought hit me: *If I want these guys to hire me, I can't sell my product. I have to sell their product.*

I pivoted on the spot. Instead of pitching DRIVE, I built a Value Stack—positioning Frazer and Rob as the absolute best investment this audience could make.

- I highlighted their success: Multi-seven-figure earners.
- I reinforced their credibility: The most influential voices in the industry.
- I had the audience say it themselves: "What have you learned from them? How has this event impacted your business?"

Within minutes, the entire room was in agreement—Frazer and Rob had changed their lives. Then I asked the money question: "By a show of hands, how many of you have signed up for their mastermind?"

Ten hands. Out of a room of 400 people, that was it.

In twenty-four hours, with all the influence these two had, only ten people had bought. I knew Frazer and Rob were building up to a massive close at the end of the event, but this was my moment to break through the noise.

I jumped off the stage. I walked into the audience. Then, I climbed onto a chair. "I am going to sell the living daylights out of every single one of you in this room!"

The crowd roared.

"I am not affiliated with their product," I clarified. "I don't make a dime off their sales. But I want you to know how it feels to be sold based on your DRIVE."

Then, I turned the entire room into a real-time case study.

"Directors," I continued, "stand up. You crave freedom. You don't want limits, restrictions, or someone telling you how to run your business. You're here because you refuse to follow a path someone else paved—you want to create your own. This mastermind will help you think bigger, move faster, and break boundaries so you can build your business on your terms."

I addressed the next buying language. "Relators, now you can stand up. You don't care about algorithms or sales funnels—you care about people. This mastermind will connect you to the biggest leaders in the industry, help you serve your team better, and deepen your relationships in ways you've never imagined."

I paused for a moment, then said, "Intellectuals, it's your turn to stand up. You're here for systems, structure, and efficiency. You want proven frameworks. Frazer and Rob have the most advanced, battle-tested strategies in direct sales. Their mastermind will help you optimize, organize, and scale faster than you ever could on your own."

Then, someone shouted from the back of the room, "Will you quit talking and just take my damn credit card already?"

The crowd exploded with laughter, but I wasn't done.

"Validators," I continued. "Please stand up. You know what this mastermind gives you? Status. Recognition. Being connected to the two biggest leaders in the industry makes you the go-to leader in your space. Imagine the respect you'll earn when you bring these strategies back to your team."

I reached the final DRIVE and said, "Executives, stand up. You don't need me to convince you. You already know who these two are. They're the best of the best. You're here because you want to win. The only question left is: Are you ready to stop waiting and start executing?"

The room was on fire.

Then, I drove urgency home. "If you buy in the next twenty-four hours, I will personally do a one-hour DRIVE training for all of you—for free."

The results? By the end of lunch, they had thirty new orders—a 300% increase in sales. Within twenty-four hours? 144 people bought in. That's a 1,440% increase in sales.

After the event, Rob pulled me aside and told me, "While you were closing, Frazer turned to me and asked, 'Do you think I can convince Woody to train at my UK event?'"

I was elated. Not only did I train in the UK—I've since trained for Frazer in Germany, Portugal, and Dubai.

The Platinum Rule:
The Key to Selling the Way People Want to Buy

We've all heard of the Golden Rule: "Do unto others as you would like them to do unto you." But in sales, that mindset is actually selfish. It means you're treating others—or selling to them—based on your own DRIVE rather than theirs.

Instead, the most successful salespeople follow the Platinum Rule, coined by Dr. Tony Alessandra: "Do unto others the way they want to be done unto." In other words, treat people the way they want to be treated—by speaking *their* buying language, not yours.

Sales isn't about persuasion. It's about alignment. When you learn to sell in a way that aligns with your client's DRIVE, everything changes. Sales conversations stop feeling like an uphill battle. Clients engage more. Objections disappear. Closing feels like a conversation. When you speak their language, you don't have to convince anyone to buy—they already want to.

By now, I am sure you've already started seeing sales differently. But we're just getting started. Before you can master the perfect pitch that resonates with your client's DRIVE, you first need to discover your own.

3

Discover Your DRIVE

What separates the best in the world from everyone else? It's not luck, talent, or education—it's the way they are wired. Jeff Bezos, Oprah Winfrey, Thomas Edison, Serena Williams, and Steve Jobs didn't just succeed; they operated from an internal engine that dictated their every move. You have the same power source inside of you. The question is—are you using it to its full potential?

Every top performer moves differently. They don't hesitate. They don't second-guess. They don't rely on motivation—they rely on something deeper. This isn't willpower, discipline, or mindset. This is your DRIVE. It's as fundamental to your success as your fingerprint is to your identity.

How well you tap into and harness your DRIVE determines whether you soar or stagnate. This isn't solely about sales—it's about standing out as a force in your industry, commanding respect, and performing at an elite level. When you understand your DRIVE, you gain a level of resilience and purpose that separates the mediocre from the unstoppable. It's what makes some people lead, innovate, and dominate, while others coast, conform, and fade into the background. Knowing what truly fuels you transforms how you work, how you influence, and how you connect with others. This is the undeniable power of DRIVE.

Consider the following examples:

- Steve Jobs was driven by relentless perfectionism and innovation. His DRIVE led him to revolutionize multiple industries, from personal computing to mobile technology.
- Dwayne "The Rock" Johnson is fueled by resilience and reinvention. His DRIVE took him from an uncertain football career to dominating professional wrestling, Hollywood, and business.
- Sara Blakely was motivated by sheer determination and problem-solving. Her DRIVE turned a $5,000 investment into Spanx, making her one of the youngest self-made billionaires.
- Kobe Bryant was obsessed with mastery. His DRIVE to outwork and outthink any and all competition made him one of the most legendary players in NBA history.
- Vera Wang is fueled by an obsessive DRIVE for innovation and artistry. She redefined bridal fashion, turning gowns into statements of style and sophistication, constantly pushing the boundaries of design.
- Howard Schultz was driven by vision and leadership. His DRIVE transformed Starbucks from a small coffee retailer into a global powerhouse.

Patterns of success exist everywhere. Consider how a stand-up comedian can make an audience laugh with only a microphone and an empty stage, or how a chess grandmaster can defeat an opponent using the same sixteen pieces everyone starts with. The most extraordinary achievements come from mastering the fundamentals and pushing them to their highest level.

The same principles apply to technology and innovation. Every digital device you use, from your smartphone to artificial intelligence, operates on just two numbers—zero and one. With that simple binary code, we've created entire industries, revolutionized communication, and connected the world in ways previously unimaginable.

Human behavior is no different. It may seem complex, but at its core, there are fundamental drivers that shape every decision, action, and success story. This is where DRIVE comes in. Much like how a painter turns basic colors into masterpieces or an architect transforms simple geometric shapes into skyscrapers, your DRIVE is the raw material that, when harnessed correctly, leads to extraordinary outcomes.

Discovering Your DRIVE

You might be wondering, "How is DRIVE different from other personality profiles like Myers-Briggs™, DiSC™, or 16 Personalities™?"

Simple. DRIVE isn't another personality quiz—it's your blueprint for unlocking what fuels you at your core. Traditional personality tests put you in a box based on traits, behaviors, or communication styles. DRIVE shatters that box. It reveals *why* you do what you do—and *how* you do it.

This isn't about surface tendencies. It's about the defining moments—the dramatic and the traumatic—that have shaped you. Unlike static personality types, DRIVE is alive. It moves with you, grows with your ambitions, and sharpens as you gain self-awareness.

Understanding your DRIVE isn't just self-discovery—it's accessing your unfair advantage. When you know what fuels you, you play the game differently. You make sharper decisions, build deeper connections, and get results at a level most people will never touch.

This process isn't about ego. It's not about chasing status, approval, or recognition. It's about the one thing at your core that makes you feel truly alive. That moment when you're in your zone—when you feel seen, valued, and unstoppable. Every human being needs this. And the more you understand what makes you *feel* important, the more control you have over your success.

This innate desire for importance drives your decisions, shapes your actions, and defines your purpose. In *How to Win Friends and Influence People*, Dale Carnegie dedicated an entire chapter to this concept, highlighting its profound impact:

"There is one all-important law of human conduct. If we obey that law, we shall almost never get into trouble. In fact, that law, if obeyed, will bring us countless friends and constant happiness. But the very instant we break the law, we shall get into endless trouble. The law is this: Always make the other person feel important."

At its essence, DRIVE isn't about competition—it's about unlocking what makes you unique and unstoppable. The better you understand what fuels you, the more control you have over your success.

Discovering Your DRIVE: An Interactive Journey

Your DRIVE is already impacting your life, whether you realize it or not. The question is: Are you tapping into it or leaving your full potential untapped?

Go to **www.WhatIsMyDRIVE.com** and take the assessment now. In just five minutes, this simple 35-question survey will uncover what truly drives you. Once you see it, you'll never look at yourself—or your success—the same way again.

But don't stop there. Once you've completed the assessment, come back to this book to explore your results in depth. Understanding your DRIVE is just the beginning. Now that you have a glimpse of what fuels your actions and decisions, it's time to unlock the unique personalities that DRIVE embodies.

In the next chapters, we'll break down each DRIVE type, helping you recognize not only your own but also those around you. This knowledge will deepen your connections, strengthen your influence, and elevate your success—in business, relationships, and beyond.

DRIVE Overview:
How to Navigate Chapter 4

Now that you've discovered your Primary and Secondary DRIVE, it's time to make this journey personal.

To keep things focused and save you time, the next five sections break down each DRIVE type:

Primary DRIVE:

- D—Director (pg. 33)
- R—Relator (pg. 41)
- I—Intellectual (pg. 51)
- V—Validator (pg. 59)
- E—Executive (pg. 67)

For now, zero in on your **Primary DRIVE.** This part will give you the most immediate and powerful insight into what motivates you, how you make decisions, and what truly drives your success.

Once you've finished the book, come back and explore the other DRIVE types. You'll gain the ability to connect, lead, and sell more effectively by recognizing what motivates your friends, family, coworkers, and clients at their core.

For now, it's time to focus on you. Because when you understand what drives you, you unlock your full potential.

Let's get started.

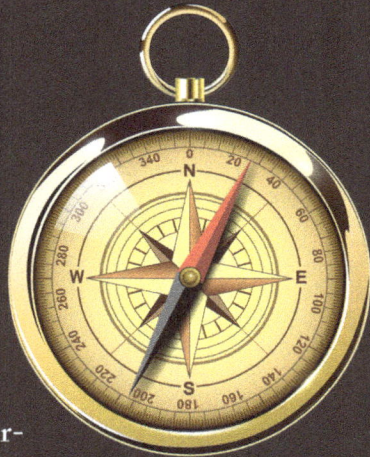

Director: The Visionary Trailblazer

You were born to lead, not follow the crowd.

You don't just dream of a better future—you create it. You thrive in motion, in challenges, in the thrill of forging your own path. Limits? Restrictions? Bureaucracy? They suffocate you. You were built to stand out.

A Director DRIVE isn't just about ambition—it also encompasses freedom, independence, and the relentless pursuit of something bigger than yourself. Whether you're launching businesses, pioneering new ideas, or breaking boundaries in your industry, you move differently.

You don't wait for permission.

You don't play it safe.

You don't settle.

And when the world tells you to slow down?

You push even harder.

For Directors, fulfillment comes from three core pursuits:

- **Freedom**—Living life on your own terms, making decisions without limits.

- **Conquering Challenges**—Overcoming obstacles and proving what's possible.

- **Creative Expression**—Whether it's in business, fashion, art, or leadership, you thrive when you're creating something only you could have built.

Personal Life: Living Life on Your Terms

For you, life isn't meant to be lived according to someone else's rules. You need space to think, move, and create without feeling boxed in. Routine and predictability drain you—your energy comes from possibility, spontaneity, and the freedom to follow your instincts.

You don't wait for the perfect plan; you trust yourself to figure it out as you go. Some people need structure to feel safe—you need movement to feel alive.

Your best moments happen when you're steering your own life, free to explore, create, and take action on your own terms. You don't always know where the road leads, but that's the thrill. You move forward, trusting that whatever comes next, you'll handle it. Because you always do.

Relationships: Freedom to Connect

For you, connection thrives in an atmosphere of trust, space, and mutual freedom. You're drawn to people who bring energy and excitement—those who can keep up with your ideas, embrace spontaneity, and push beyond the ordinary. Whether it's a partner, friend, or colleague, the best relationships fuel your sense of endless possibility, not restrict it.

You show love through shared experiences—inviting others into your world and encouraging them to step outside their comfort zones. Nothing excites you more than people who are willing to explore life without holding you back.

What drains you? Clinginess, neediness, and control. You can't stand being micromanaged or pressured into rigid expectations. When someone constantly seeks reassurance, places emotional demands on you, or tries to dictate your path, it creates instant tension. You value connection, but not at the expense of your independence.

The right relationships don't confine you—they amplify you. When you find people who respect your nature, you become a force of inspiration, creativity, and movement. With the right people by your side, you're at your best—always moving forward, never stuck in the ordinary.

Career: Leading the Charge

You don't merely work—you build, create, and challenge the way things are done. Routine tasks and rigid systems don't motivate you; possibility does. You thrive in careers that give you the freedom to pursue big ideas, take bold risks, and make an impact on your own terms. Whether you're an entrepreneur, a visionary leader, or the driving force behind innovation, you excel when you have the space to push boundaries and shape your own path.

For you, challenges are opportunities to prove what's possible. You move fast, think big, and refuse to settle for "good enough." The moment creativity is stifled, decisions slow down. When unnecessary rules get in the way, frustration sets in. Sitting in endless meetings with no action? Unbearable. You thrive on momentum, and when others hesitate, you're already ten steps ahead.

That's why you do your best work when you're leading the charge, setting the vision, making bold moves, and turning ideas into reality. For you, success isn't about following a formula—it's about writing your own.

A Director's Motto:

"The people who are crazy enough to think they can change the world are the ones who do."

—Steve Jobs

Examples of Successful Directors:

- Larry Page (Co-Founder, Google)
- Dr. Dre (Co-Founder, Beats by Dre)
- Melanie Perkins (Co-Founder & CEO, Canva)
- Hans Wilsdorf (Founder, Rolex)
- Reese Witherspoon (Actress, Producer, Founder of Hello Sunshine)
- Joe Rogan (Podcaster & Media Personality)
- Barbara Corcoran (Real Estate Mogul, Shark Tank Investor)
- Lorne Michaels (Creator & Executive Producer, Saturday Night Live)

Daniel Ek:
The Director Who Rewrote the Music Industry

A Director doesn't wait for permission. A Director doesn't follow the rules, either. They rip them up and rewrite them. And no one embodies this DRIVE better than Daniel Ek.

In the early 2000s, the music industry was a disaster. CDs were dying, piracy was thriving, and the record labels were clinging to a broken system. The industry's so-called "leaders" were too afraid to evolve. Most people saw an unsolvable problem. Ek saw an opportunity.

At twenty-three years old, he did what Directors do best: he looked past the limitations and saw the future before anyone else. The industry was built on the belief that people wanted to own music. Ek knew better. People didn't care about ownership— they wanted access.

Any song, anytime, anywhere. But making that happen? That meant taking on an entire industry dead set on stopping him.

The pushback was brutal. Record labels laughed him out of the room. Investors called him insane. Lawsuits loomed like storm clouds. Any reasonable person would have backed down, but Directors aren't reasonable.

Instead of folding, Ek doubled down. He obsessed over every detail. He spent years locked in negotiations no one thought he could win. He fought. He adapted. He refused to let an outdated system dictate the future.

Then, in 2008, Spotify launched—and the world never listened to music the same way again.

Ek didn't follow a roadmap. He made his own. When the world says, "That's not how it's done," a Director chooses to break the mold and take the lead.

But here's the truth about being a Director: it's a blessing and a burden.

Ek's story proves what every Director already knows—waiting is agony. Watching people cling to old systems drives you insane. And when people don't see your vision? You push forward anyway.

Because for a Director, there's no Plan B. If the path doesn't exist, there's only one option: build it.

Let's take a closer look at the challenges that Directors can face, as well as the strengths they possess.

Weaknesses of Directors:

- **Impatience with Complaints:** Directors can sometimes be unsympathetic to those who complain, preferring action over negativity.
- **Self-Critical About Appearance:** They can be excessively hard on themselves regarding their appearance and presentation.

- **Challenges in Team Dynamics:** Their strong personalities and independent nature can sometimes result in a lack of teamwork.

- **Frustration Over Unrecognized Creativity:** Directors may feel frustrated when others do not value or understand their creative input.

- **Disappointment in Unmet Goals:** Not achieving their life's purpose can deeply disappoint them.

- **Impulsiveness:** Their spontaneity can be difficult for others to keep up with.

- **Risk of Burnout:** Their tendency to try to do everything can lead to exhaustion.

Strengths of Directors:

- **Creative and Passionate:** Directors are inherently outgoing about their endeavors. Their zest infuses innovation and excitement into their projects.

- **Spontaneous and Adventurous:** They approach life with enthusiasm and adventure, always ready to explore new opportunities.

- **Expressive and Stylish:** Naturally fashionable, Directors carry themselves with an unmistakable confidence.

- **Resilient and Optimistic:** They are known for their eternal ability to look on the bright side, never giving up even in the face of adversity.

- **Strong-Willed and Visionary:** Directors are determined and willing to make sacrifices to achieve their goals.

- **Open-Minded:** Their ability to think outside the box allows them to come up with innovative solutions to complex problems.

Selling to Directors: Speak to Their Vision

To sell effectively to a Director, you need to match their energy, respect their independence, and speak to their vision. Directors aren't just looking for solutions—they're looking for tools to help them break new ground, move faster, and create on their own terms. They're drawn to products and services that enhance their autonomy, fuel their creativity, and give them the power to shape their own future.

Be direct, be confident, and don't waste their time. A Director respects boldness. Show them how what you're offering isn't just useful—it's a game-changer. Emphasize innovation, efficiency, and the ability to disrupt outdated methods. Make it clear that your solution is about pushing boundaries and helping them take the lead.

More than anything, Directors want to see how your solution amplifies their experience. They're not buying a product; they're investing in a tool that helps them create, innovate, and win on their own terms. If you can connect your offering to their bigger vision—their ability to shape industries, redefine success, or chase what excites them—you'll have their full attention.

And be sure to showcase what the product allows them to do. When you recognize their ability to think ahead, take risks, and drive change, you're not just making a sale—you're building trust. Speak to their DRIVE, and they'll trust you to help them conquer what's next.

If this is your first time reading about your Primary DRIVE, skip the other four and jump straight to Chapter 5 (pg. 77). Once you've finished the book, come back and explore the other DRIVEs to better understand how they impact your customers, clients, and teams. For now, let's see how DRIVE shows up when millions of dollars—and egos—are on the line.

Relator: The Master Connector

You don't just meet people—you truly connect with them. Relationships are the heartbeat of your world, and your ability to understand, uplift, and bring people together is unmatched. Whether it's guiding a team, supporting a friend, or strengthening family bonds, you thrive when your presence makes a lasting impact.

For you, influence isn't about power—it's about connection. You live for the moments where someone feels seen because of you, where trust is built, and where lives are changed through relationships. You don't just build networks; you create communities. You naturally forge deep bonds that stand the test of time.

Your fulfillment comes from three core channels:

- **Influence, relationships, family, friends, and parenting**—The people in your life aren't just important; they are everything.

- **Giving, serving, and volunteering**—Making a difference is essential to who you are.

- **Spirituality (as defined by you)**—Whether through faith, purpose, or a sense of belonging, you seek deeper meaning in life and in your connections.

Personal Life: Living Through Connection

For you, life is an open invitation to experience, to feel, to connect. You don't just go through the motions; you immerse yourself in the moments that matter. Whether it's the warmth of a familiar place, the comfort of a cherished tradition, or the simple joy of shared laughter, your world is built around the energy of connection.

You find fulfillment in meaningful experiences, not only milestones. A quiet morning of gratitude and reflection, the joy of storytelling, or even the nostalgia of revisiting an old memory—these are the essence of life itself.

You naturally create an atmosphere where people feel welcome, but beyond that, you cultivate a life that feels rich with emotion, depth, and purpose. Whether through music, books, or art, you gravitate toward things that stir your soul.

For you, success isn't just about what you do; it's about how deeply you feel, experience, and connect.

Relationships: The Power of Connection

For you, relationships are about surrounding yourself with meaningful connection. You invest deeply in others, and your presence makes people feel seen, heard, and valued. Whether in friendships, family, or romance, you bring warmth, loyalty, and a genuine desire to support those you care about.

Nothing frustrates you more than feeling unappreciated, excluded, or disconnected. You struggle with relationships that lack emotional depth, where people are distant, dismissive, or unwilling to reciprocate the effort you put in. When communication breaks down or your feelings are overlooked, it weighs heavily on you—because for you, true connection is essential.

But when you're surrounded by people who value and nurture your bond, you flourish. You bring depth, understanding, and unwavering support, creating relationships that are built to last. With the right people, you form connections that stand the test of time and transform the lives that you touch.

Career: Purpose Through People

For you, work isn't just about tasks and results—it's about people. You thrive in careers where relationships, collaboration, and trust-building take center stage. Whether leading a team, mentoring colleagues, or working with clients, your ability to understand and connect with others gives you a natural advantage. You create an environment where people feel valued, motivated, and inspired to do their best work.

But nothing drains you faster than cold, transactional workplaces or environments where people are treated as numbers instead of individuals. Office politics, toxic cultures, or rigid systems that put processes above humanity can leave you feeling unfulfilled. When appreciation fades and collaboration is replaced by competition, work begins to feel hollow.

Whether in leadership, sales, coaching, or any team-driven profession, your ability to connect and bring people together makes you invaluable. When your work allows you to authentically make a difference, it doesn't feel like a job—it feels like a calling.

A Relator's Motto:

"People will forget what you said, people will forget what you did, but people will never forget how you made them feel."

— *Maya Angelou*

Examples of Successful Relators:

- Blake Mycoskie (Founder, TOMS Shoes)
- Taylor Swift (Singer-Songwriter & Businesswoman)
- Charles & Jean Stern (Owners, Patek Philippe)
- Tyler Perry (Filmmaker, Actor, & Playwright)
- Oprah Winfrey (Oprah Winfrey Network)
- Fred Rogers (Creator, Mister Rogers' Neighborhood)
- Martin Luther King Jr. (Civil Rights Leader & Minister)
- Ryan Reynolds (Actor, Co-Owner, Aviation Gin & Mint Mobile)

Andrew Cherng:
The Heart That Built an Empire

A Relator doesn't chase success for themselves. A Relator builds something for others—something that brings people together, something that matters. And no one embodies that better than Andrew Cherng.

When he co-founded Panda Express, he chose to build a family. From day one, his vision wasn't about selling food. It was about creating a place where people felt seen, valued, and cared for. A place where employees weren't just workers but part of something bigger.

Most entrepreneurs focus on profits. Cherng focused on people.

While other fast-food chains chased speed and automation, he doubled down on relationships. The industry saw employees as replaceable. Cherng saw potential. He believed a business wasn't just about the product—it was about the culture behind

it. If he took care of his employees, they would take care of the customers.

So he invested in them by offering leadership training and personal development programs. His company culture was built on genuine care and the kind of commitment no one else in the industry was making.

The result? A company that didn't just thrive—it flourished.

But being a Relator in business isn't easy.

Investors wanted aggressive expansion. Industry experts dismissed his people-first approach as a waste of resources. They told him fast food was about efficiency. They didn't understand.

Cherng knew the truth—real success isn't just measured in revenue. It's measured in impact. He was giving people careers, not just jobs. He was creating a space where employees felt empowered, where customers felt welcomed, and where something as simple as sharing a meal became more.

And it worked.

Panda Express grew into the largest Asian-segment restaurant chain in the United States, with over 2,400 locations.

This is what a Relator's DRIVE looks like. They don't dominate through competition—they win through connection. They build something bigger than themselves.

For a Relator, business is about belonging. And when they get it right, they don't just build businesses.

They build legacies.

Let's take a closer look at the challenges that Relators can face, as well as the strengths they possess.

Weaknesses of Relators:

- **Overly Empathetic:** Relators can sometimes become too emotionally involved in others' issues, which may lead to personal stress or decision-making that's overly influenced by emotions rather than logic.

- **Difficulty with Boundaries:** Due to their nurturing nature, Relators might struggle to set and enforce personal and professional boundaries, often at the cost of their own well-being.

- **Avoidance of Conflict:** Their strong desire for harmony can make Relators avoid necessary confrontations, which can lead to unresolved issues in teams or relationships.

- **High Expectations of Others:** Relators often expect the same level of emotional engagement and commitment they offer, which can lead to disappointment when others do not meet these expectations.

- **Risk of Being Taken Advantage Of:** Their willingness to help and connect can sometimes be exploited by less scrupulous individuals.

- **Reluctance to Change:** Relators may prefer maintaining established relationships and routines, sometimes resisting new ideas or practices that could disrupt their sense of community.

Strengths of Relators:

- **Empathetic and Compassionate:** Relators excel in understanding and sharing the feelings of others, which enhances their ability to connect deeply.

- **Great Communicators:** They are often skilled at expressing themselves and navigating conversations that require tact and sensitivity.

- **Loyal and Supportive:** Relators are known for their faithfulness and are often the pillars within their communities and organizations.

- **Influential in Team Environments:** Their ability to understand and relate to others makes them natural leaders in team settings, fostering a collaborative and inclusive atmosphere.

- **Intuitive:** Relators have a strong intuition about the emotions and needs of others, which can guide their decisions and interactions effectively.
- **Dedicated to Service:** With a strong drive to help and serve, Relators often thrive in roles that allow them to contribute positively to the lives of others.

Selling to Relators: Build Genuine Connections

Understanding the strengths and challenges of Relators allows you to craft a sales approach that truly speaks to them. Relators are drawn to products and services that enhance relationships, strengthen communities, and foster deeper connections. If what you're offering helps them support, uplift, or bring people together, they'll listen.

When selling to a Relator, lead with sincerity and warmth. They are not transactional buyers—they seek meaningful engagement. Show them how your product or service builds trust or contributes positively to their world. More than features, they want to understand how your solution supports what they care about most—people.

Relators feel most valued when their role as a connector is recognized. If you acknowledge their dedication to relationships, you're not just making a sale—you're reinforcing their identity as someone who makes a difference. The stronger the emotional connection, the stronger the trust.

At their core, Relators want to uplift others. If you align your sales strategy with this motivation, you turn a conversation into a partnership. Speak to their DRIVE, and they won't just buy from you—they'll become loyal advocates for what you offer.

If this is your first time reading about your Primary DRIVE, skip the other four and jump straight to Chapter 5 (pg. 77). Once you've finished the book, come back and explore the other DRIVEs to better understand how they impact your customers, clients, and teams. For now, let's see how DRIVE shows up when millions of dollars—and egos—are on the line.

.

Intellectual: The Strategic Thinker

You are the type of person who must analyze, question, and refine. The world isn't a series of random events; it's a system waiting to be understood, optimized, and improved. Your mind is always breaking things down, searching for patterns, and uncovering the deeper truths beneath the surface. Others may be satisfied with simple answers, but for you, there's always a why—and you won't stop until you find it.

You don't chase knowledge for the sake of trivia but for the pursuit of mastery. Learning is about understanding how things work and making them better. Whether it's solving a complex problem, designing a more efficient system, or challenging outdated ideas, you thrive when your intellect is fully engaged. You don't accept things as they are—you push for what they could be.

Your DRIVE is fulfilled through three core channels:

- **Pursuit of knowledge and learning**—Every answer leads to a new question, and that's exactly how you like it.

- **High standards and organization**—Structure and precision are necessities. Excellence isn't optional—it's the only way forward.

- **Being present in nature and prioritizing health**—Clarity comes when distractions fade. Whether through time in nature, movement, or mindful reflection, you recognize the connection between a sharp mind and a balanced life.

Personal Life: A Life of Thought and Discovery

For you, life is a constant search for understanding, depth, and insight. You aren't satisfied with just knowing *what*—you need to know *why*. Whether it's philosophy, science, psychology, or personal development, you thrive when your mind is engaged, uncovering new perspectives and refining your understanding of the world.

You find fulfillment in meaningful, thought-provoking conversations. Small talk and surface-level interactions feel empty because you crave exchanges that challenge ideas, introduce fresh concepts, and spark curiosity. Whether you're debating theories, analyzing problems, or absorbing knowledge, your world expands when learning is at its center.

Your mind is always reaching, always questioning, always growing. For you, fulfillment isn't found in the familiar—it's discovered in the pursuit of what's next.

Relationships: The Power of Thoughtful Connection

For you, relationships are about exploring ideas, exchanging perspectives, and growing through conversation. You connect best with people who are curious, open-minded, and willing to challenge their own thinking. Whether in friendships, family, or romance, you value intellectual compatibility—a relationship where depth, logic, and meaningful discussion are the foundation.

Nothing frustrates you more than shallow conversations, emotional drama, or rigid thinking. You struggle with people who reject logic, make decisions purely on feelings, or dismiss curiosity. You also need mental space—constant social demands or emotional intensity can feel overwhelming when you haven't had time to reflect and process your thoughts.

But when you find relationships that respect your need for depth, autonomy, and mental stimulation, you thrive. You bring wisdom, insight, and a perspective that helps others see the world in new ways. Your ability to think deeply and solve problems makes you a trusted advisor, a loyal friend, and someone whose presence adds clarity and meaning to the lives of those around you.

Career: Mastery Through Knowledge

For you, work isn't just about completing tasks—it's about understanding, improving, and mastering complex systems. You thrive in environments where critical thinking, problem-solving, and continuous learning are not only valued but expected. Whether you're analyzing data, developing strategies, or refining processes, you operate best when your mind is fully engaged. You love deepening your expertise and pushing boundaries.

Few things frustrate you more than mindless repetition or intellectual stagnation. Workplaces that avoid critical thinking drain your energy. Office politics, emotional decision-making, or environments resistant to change can leave you feeling disconnected. You need space to question, refine, and optimize—because progress isn't made by accepting things as they are.

That's why you excel in careers that reward intelligence, strategy, and innovation. Whether in research, technology, consulting, or leadership, your ability to think critically, solve problems, and drive meaningful change makes you invaluable. When your work challenges you, it's more than a career—it's a lifelong pursuit of mastery and discovery.

An Intellectual's Motto:

"An investment in knowledge pays the best interest."

—*Benjamin Franklin*

Examples of Successful Intellectuals:

- Albert Einstein (Theoretical Physicist)
- Anne Wojcicki (Co-Founder & CEO, 23andMe)
- Bill Gates (Co-Founder, Microsoft)
- Whitney Wolfe Herd (Founder & CEO, Bumble)
- Bill Lear (Founder, Learjet)
- Ursula Burns (Former CEO, Xerox)
- Fred Smith (Founder & CEO, FedEx)
- Susan Wojcicki (Former CEO, YouTube)

Jan Koum:
The Thinker Who Connected the World

An Intellectual isn't driven by status. They're not chasing applause, power, or prestige. They're driven by one thing: understanding. They see problems others ignore. They obsess over solutions. And no one embodies that better than Jan Koum.

Born in Ukraine, Koum grew up knowing what it meant to be unheard. When his family immigrated to the U.S. at age sixteen, they survived on food stamps while he taught himself programming from library books. He wasn't trying to get rich—he was trying to learn.

And that obsession led him to a problem no one else was solving.

In 2009, digital communication was broken. Text messaging was expensive. International calls were unreliable. Social media was a mess of ads and noise. People didn't want more dis-tractions—they wanted connection.

Koum envisioned an app that was fast, secure, and private. No ads. No gimmicks. Just seamless, encrypted messaging. He and his co-founder, Brian Acton, built WhatsApp with an obsessive commitment to simplicity.

At first, no one cared. Investors weren't interested. Competitors dismissed it. But Intellectuals don't build for approval—they build because they see what others don't.

Koum refined, tested, and improved WhatsApp relentlessly. He refused to compromise on privacy, ensuring messages were end-to-end encrypted so no one—not even WhatsApp—could read them. His quiet persistence paid off. Within a few years, WhatsApp became the go-to messaging app worldwide.

Then, in 2014, Facebook acquired WhatsApp for $19 billion. But for Koum, success was never about the money. When Facebook pushed to monetize WhatsApp with ads and weaken its privacy protections, Koum walked away. He left nearly $1 billion in unvested stock options on the table because his principles mattered more than a paycheck.

This is the essence of an Intellectual. They don't just accept the world as it is—they reengineer it. They think deeper, push further, and refuse to compromise their vision.

But Koum's story also highlights the challenges of being an Intellectual. The frustration of being misunderstood. The isolation that comes with thinking differently. The pain of watching the world move toward profit over principles.

Because for an Intellectual, the real battle isn't just solving problems. It's making the world see what they see.

Let's take a closer look at the challenges that Intellectuals can face, as well as the strengths they possess.

Weaknesses of Intellectuals:

- **Analysis Paralysis:** Intellectuals can sometimes become so caught up in analyzing the details that decision-making may be delayed or hindered.
- **Overly Critical:** Their high standards and analytical nature can make them excessively critical of both themselves and others,

potentially stifling creativity.

- **May Struggle With Detachment:** Intellectuals might focus more on data and facts than on people's feelings, which can impact interpersonal relationships.
- **Perfectionism:** Their pursuit of perfection can lead to frustration when perfectly rational solutions are impractical or unachievable.
- **Resistance to Intuition:** Intellectuals may dismiss gut feelings in favor of analysis, which can sometimes lead to missed opportunities.
- **Social Isolation:** Their intense focus on their intellectual pursuits can sometimes lead to social isolation or difficulty in social settings.

Strengths of Intellectuals:

- **Analytical and Objective:** Intellectuals excel in situations that require critical thinking and problem-solving, using their analytical skills to navigate complex issues.
- **Innovative:** They are often at the forefront of innovation, using their knowledge to create new theories, products, or solutions.
- **Inquisitive:** Intellectuals have a natural curiosity that drives continuous learning and exploration, keeping them well-informed and prepared.
- **Strategic Thinkers:** They are excellent at seeing the big picture and planning strategically to achieve long-term goals.
- **Detail-Oriented:** Intellectuals' attention to detail ensures thoroughness in tasks, research, and projects.
- **Effective Communicators:** They are often able to clearly articulate complex ideas and theories, making them valuable in roles that require teaching or presenting sophisticated concepts.

Selling to Intellectuals: Engage Their Mind

Intellectuals don't make impulsive decisions—they analyze, evaluate, and seek logic-backed solutions. To sell effectively to them, your approach must be clear, data-driven, and intellectually compelling. They are drawn to efficiency, innovation, and deep understanding, so surface-level pitches won't work. They want substance, not fluff.

When presenting your product or service, emphasize how it enhances their knowledge, optimizes systems, or pushes the boundaries of conventional thinking. Show them the research, the logic, and the evidence-based advantages. They don't buy hype—they buy proof. If your offering can make something smarter, faster, or more effective, make that case with precision.

Intellectuals take pride in their ability to discern quality and think critically. Acknowledge their expertise, respect their analytical nature, and provide them with meaningful insights. If they walk away feeling like they've learned something valuable from you, you're on the right track.

At their core, Intellectuals are driven by a relentless pursuit of knowledge and mastery. If your sales approach aligns with that motivation, they won't just consider your solution—they'll analyze it, test it, and, if it holds up, adopt it. Because for an Intellectual, trust is earned through clarity, logic, and verification.

If this is your first time reading about your Primary DRIVE, skip the other four and jump straight to Chapter 5 (pg. 77). Once you've finished the book, come back and explore the other DRIVEs to better understand how they impact your customers, clients, and teams. For now, let's see how DRIVE shows up when millions of dollars—and egos—are on the line.

Validator: The Trusted Foundation

For you, success isn't just about what you accomplish—it's about knowing your contributions matter. You work hard and invest yourself fully. You give your best because you take pride in what you do. But what fuels you isn't simply achievement—it's recognition, respect, and trust built from within and from those around you.

You thrive when people see your strengths, respect your judgment, and appreciate your efforts. You don't seek attention for the sake of it—you desire validation that your work, your choices, and your presence make an impact. Whether in work, relationships, or personal pursuits, you operate at your highest level when you feel valued, confident, and trusted.

Your sense of worth is deeply connected to the difference you make—for yourself and those around you. You build stability. You bring reliability. You are the foundation that others count on.

Your DRIVE is fulfilled through three core channels:

- **Trust and respect**—When you trust your instincts and stand by your judgment, you command respect—both from yourself and others.

- **Impact and recognition**—Knowing your contributions make a difference reinforces your confidence and momentum.

- **Being valued and relied upon**—You thrive when your expertise and presence play a key role in something greater than yourself.

Personal Life: The Standard You Set

For you, life is about excellence, integrity, and personal growth. You take pride in your ability to master skills, uphold high standards, and strive to be the best version of yourself. Whether it's through your work, personal achievements, or the principles you live by, you feel most fulfilled when you know you're living up to your own expectations.

You don't cut corners and you don't settle for mediocrity. When you set a goal, you commit fully—not because anyone is watching, but because you hold yourself to an unbreakable higher standard. You are your own toughest critic and greatest motivator.

For you, success is about the inner confidence that comes from knowing you've earned every bit of it. When you trust yourself, rely on your judgment, and see the tangible impact of your efforts, you don't just feel validated—you feel unstoppable.

Relationships: The Strength of Being Valued

For you, relationships are built on respect, trust, and genuine appreciation. You invest deeply in the people who notice your strengths, recognize your efforts, and acknowledge your contributions. Loyalty isn't just something you give—it's something you expect in return. When someone values you, you naturally support, encourage, and lift them up, helping them reach their full potential as well.

But nothing wounds you more than feeling dismissed, unappreciated, or taken for granted. You struggle with people who ignore your input, overlook your effort, or fail to recognize what you bring to the relationship. Criticism without acknowledgment feels like rejection, and broken trust can shake your sense of belonging. When respect is missing, so is your motivation to stay invested.

However, when you're surrounded by people who genuinely respect and appreciate you, you thrive. You bring confidence, wisdom, and unwavering support, making you someone others deeply depend on. You are the 4 a.m. friend—the one people call when they need someone reliable and true. Your word is solid and your presence brings certainty in uncertain moments. When you feel truly seen and valued, your relationships aren't just strong—they are unshakable, built on a foundation that stands the test of time.

Career: Excellence Recognized

For you, work isn't merely completing tasks—it's a way to earn respect, prove your expertise, and know that your contributions matter. You take pride in what you do, not just for personal success, but because you want to be seen as competent, trusted, and valuable. Whether you're leading a team, perfecting a skill, or making key decisions, you thrive when your effort is recognized and your input is respected.

Few things frustrate you more than being overlooked, undervalued, or treated as if your work doesn't matter. You struggle in environments where leadership ignores employee contributions, credit is unfairly given, or hard work goes unnoticed. Disrespect and dismissiveness are frustrating and demotivating. If your value isn't acknowledged, it makes you question whether you belong at all.

That's why you excel in careers where trust, credibility, and recognition are earned and respected. Whether in leadership, consulting, customer relations, or any role that relies on expertise and integrity, you bring a level of dedication and reliability that makes you indispensable. When you're in an environment where your worth is seen and appreciated, work becomes a reflection of your impact and the respect you've earned.

A Validator's Motto:

"Respect is how to treat everyone, not just those you want to impress."
—*Richard Branson*

Examples of Successful Validators:

- Howard Schultz (Former CEO & Chairman, Starbucks)
- Maxine Clark (Founder, Build-A-Bear Workshop)
- Ole Kirk Christiansen (Founder, LEGO)
- Tamara Mellon (Co-Founder, Jimmy Choo)
- Andrew Mason (Founder, Groupon)
- Brené Brown (Researcher, Author & Speaker)
- Jack Ma (Co-Founder, Alibaba Group)
- Bert Kreischer (Comedian, Podcaster & Entertainer)

Brené Brown:
Selling Through Trust

A Validator doesn't just seek recognition—they build trust. And no one turned trust into a global brand better than Brené Brown.

For years, Brown studied human connection—what makes people feel worthy, what holds them back, and why shame has such a powerful grip on our lives. But she didn't just research these ideas; she turned them into a business model.

Then, in 2010, everything changed.

She gave a TED Talk on the power of vulnerability, expecting a small academic audience. Instead, millions watched. And something powerful happened: people didn't just admire her. They trusted her. And when people trust you, they buy from you.

Before long, her books were bestsellers. Her speaking fees skyrocketed. Companies brought her in to train leaders on trust and authenticity in business. She

was spreading a revolutionary idea and selling it. Millions of people were willing to pay a premium for it.

This is where Validators excel. People buy from those they believe in, and Brown mastered the art of selling without selling—by creating an unshakable connection with her audience. She didn't chase status but instead built influence. She didn't just publish books—she sold a new way of thinking.

But being a Validator in business isn't easy. The fear of rejection, the need for approval, and the pressure to maintain authenticity while growing a brand—these are all battles Validators must face. Brown had to learn the hardest lesson of all: external validation can get you noticed, but internal validation is what keeps you in the game.

And it worked. Her research redefined leadership, trust, and business communication. Her courses, speaking engagements, and consulting fees turned vulnerability into a multimillion-dollar enterprise. She shared her truth and brilliantly sold it at scale.

Brené Brown's journey is the perfect example of how a Validator's DRIVE isn't just about connection—it's about turning trust into influence and influence into revenue.

Let's take a closer look at the challenges that Validators can face, as well as the strengths they possess.

Weaknesses of Validators:

- **Can Be Overly Sensitive to Criticism:** Validators take feedback personally and may struggle with self-doubt if they feel unrecognized or unappreciated.
- **Seeking External Validation:** At times, they may rely on others' approval to feel confident, making them vulnerable to external opinions.
- **Difficulty Letting Go of Grudges:** Validators highly value trust and respect, so betrayal or perceived slights can linger, affecting relationships and teamwork.

- **Overcommitment to Earning Respect:** Their desire to prove themselves can lead to overworking, unnecessary stress, and a need to be seen as the authority in every situation.
- **Struggle with Decision-Making:** They may hesitate to take risks without reassurance, fearing failure will damage their credibility.
- **Avoidance of Conflict:** Validators dislike confrontations that could jeopardize their reputation or relationships, sometimes avoiding tough conversations.

Strengths of Validators:

- **Trustworthy and Credible:** Validators are highly respected for their integrity, earning the trust of those around them through consistency and reliability.
- **Detail-Oriented and Thorough:** They take pride in their work, ensuring that everything they do meets high standards and is done with precision.
- **Loyal and Dependable:** Once they commit, they are deeply dedicated to their teams, organizations, and personal relationships, always striving to support those they care about.
- **Naturally Encouraging:** Validators uplift others through recognition and praise, helping to build confidence in those around them.
- **Driven by Excellence:** They hold themselves and others to high standards, pushing for continuous improvement and mastery in their field.
- **Great at Building Trust:** Their ability to establish respect and credibility makes them strong leaders and effective team players in collaborative environments.

Selling to Validators: Earning Their Trust

Validators don't tend to buy on impulse—they buy when they trust, respect, and believe in what you're offering. For them, every decision is a reflection of their credibility, reputation, and expertise. If a product or service reinforces their value, authority, or trusted position, it immediately stands out.

When selling to Validators, prove your worth. Show them certified results, honest testimonials, and detailed insights that confirm they're making the right choice. They don't respond to hype—they respond to substance. If your offering enhances their status, strengthens their reputation, or solidifies their expertise, you've got their attention.

More than anything, Validators thrive on acknowledgment and appreciation. Recognizing their insights, expertise, and high standards during your interactions helps establish trust and deepens the connection. Sales conversations should focus on building credibility, not applying pressure. Validators need to feel respected and secure in their decision-making process.

Ultimately, Validators invest in solutions that reinforce their value to others. When your sales approach aligns with their need for recognition, trust, and excellence, you're not just making a sale—you're building a relationship based on mutual respect and appreciation. And for a Validator, that's what truly matters.

If this is your first time reading about your Primary DRIVE, skip the other four and jump straight to Chapter 5 (pg. 77). Once you've finished the book, come back and explore the other DRIVEs to better understand how they impact your customers, clients, and teams. For now, let's see how DRIVE shows up when millions of dollars—and egos—are on the line.

Executive: The Relentless Achiever

For you, winning is the only option. You don't wait for success to come to you; you go out and make it happen. Life isn't about wishful thinking—it's about strategy, execution, and results. Whether it's business, sports, or personal goals, you thrive in environments where performance matters, competition drives excellence, and there's always another level to reach.

You take pride in your ability to outthink, outwork, and outperform everyone else. Challenges aren't obstacles—they're fuel. Pressure doesn't break you—it sharpens you. While others hesitate, you're already three steps ahead, turning problems into solutions and setbacks into stepping stones. Settling? Not in your vocabulary.

Your DRIVE is fulfilled through three core channels:

- **Winning and control**—You don't follow—you lead. You don't react—you dictate the pace.
- **Work, providing, and security**—Success is about ensuring stability, dominance, and control over your future.
- **Problem-solving and achieving goals**—Every challenge is an opportunity to prove why you belong at the top.

For you, achievement isn't a destination—it's a way of life. And no matter what stands in your way, one thing is certain: you will be victorious.

Personal Life: The Drive to Succeed

For you, life isn't something to be *managed*—it's something to be mastered. You don't just dream about success; you set the goal, make the plan, and execute with precision. Whether it's fitness, finances, or personal growth, you operate with a results-driven mindset. Every move you make is intentional, every action tied to forward movement. Mediocrity isn't an option.

You track your progress, push your limits, and refuse to let distractions slow you down. Efficiency is everything. Wasted time? Unacceptable. Excuses? Irrelevant. If there's a challenge, you face it head-on, knowing that discipline and effort always lead to results.

Some may see you as intense, but that's because they don't understand your standard. You're not content with "good enough"—you're here to win, improve, and dominate every area of life. Victory isn't something you hope for—it's the direct result of the work you put in. And you wouldn't have it any other way.

Relationships: Strength in Action

For you, relationships are built on respect, trust, and shared ambition. You actively align with those who challenge, inspire, and keep pace with your drive. Loyalty is a given. When you commit, you do so fully, and you expect the same in return.

You show love through action, not words. Solving problems, providing stability, and pushing others to achieve is how you demonstrate care. If someone is in your life, it's because they've earned that place, and you invest in them by helping them become stronger and more successful.

What frustrates you? Indecisiveness, lack of follow-through, and excuses. You struggle with people who are overly emotional, easily offended, or constantly in need of reassurance. If something needs to be done, you do it—and expect the same from those around you.

But when you find people who understand and respect your DRIVE, your relationships become unshakable. You are the one others turn to in crisis, the leader who makes things happen, and the partner who pushes those you care about toward their full potential.

Career: Built to Win

At work, you take charge, set the standard, and push for results. In high-stakes environments where performance is measured, competition is fierce, and only the best rise to the top, you thrive. Leadership comes naturally because you own responsibility, make confident decisions, and refuse to accept failure as an option. Challenges are welcomed. Every obstacle is just another puzzle to solve, conquer, and move past.

But few things test your patience like inefficiency, incompetence, and people who slow things down. Bureaucracy? A waste of time. Endless meetings with no action? Infuriating. Leaders who hesitate when decisions need to be made? Unacceptable. You have no tolerance for excuses, mediocrity, or people who can't execute. If something isn't working, you fix it. If someone isn't pulling their weight, you find a way to move forward without them.

Waiting for permission? Not in your nature. You create opportunities where others see barriers, push limits where others hesitate, and drive progress when others stall. Some may call your intensity intimidating, but your ability to get results makes you indispensable. Whether you're leading a team, running your own business, or dominating your industry, one thing is certain—you play to win.

An Executive's Motto:

"Winners never quit, and quitters never win."

—*Vince Lombardi*

Examples of Successful Executives:

- Calvin Klein (Fashion Designer & Founder, Calvin Klein Inc.)
- Harriet Tubman (Abolitionist, Underground Railroad)
- Jimmy Iovine (Co-Founder, Interscope Records & Beats by Dre)
- Estée Lauder (Co-Founder, Estée Lauder Companies)
- John Paul DeJoria (Co-Founder, Patrón Tequila & Paul Mitchell)
- Martha Stewart (Founder, Martha Stewart Living Omnimedia)
- Reed Hastings (Co-Founder & Former CEO, Netflix)
- Tom Monaghan (Founder, Domino's Pizza)

Phil Knight:
The Competitor Who Built an Empire

An Executive doesn't just set goals—they crush them. They don't hope for success—they engineer it. And no one embodies that better than Phil Knight.

In 1964, Knight didn't have factories, investors, or a multimillion-dollar brand. What he had was a vision and an unrelenting will to win. He saw an opening in the market: high-quality, affordable running shoes for athletes. Most people talk about ideas. Executives act.

With a $50 loan from his father, he partnered with track coach Bill Bowerman to launch Blue Ribbon Sports. There were no stores, no big marketing budgets—only a trunk full of shoes

and Knight's refusal to lose. He drove from track meet to track meet, selling Onitsuka Tiger running shoes out of his green Plymouth Valiant. But he wasn't just selling—he was gathering intel, building relationships, and refining his game plan.

The road to success was brutal.

Cash flow crises. Legal battles. Supply chain failures. And when Onitsuka tried to cut him out of the deal, he did what Executives do best—he pivoted and went on the offensive.

In 1971, he launched his own brand: Nike.

But the war wasn't over. Adidas ruled the industry. Then, in the 1980s, Reebok surged ahead, briefly outselling Nike. For most, this would have been a knockout punch. For Knight, it was fuel. He doubled down on innovation and marketing. He didn't just sign athletes—he turned them into icons. His boldest move? Betting on a rookie named Michael Jordan.

That bet paid off.

Nike projected $3 million in Air Jordan sales over four years. Instead, they hit $126 million in the first year alone, shattering expectations.

But Knight's strategy went beyond numbers—it was about defiance. At the time, NBA rules required shoes to be predominantly white. The Air Jordans, with their bold black-and-red design, violated that rule. The NBA fined Jordan $5,000 per game for wearing them.

Knight saw this as an opportunity. Nike paid the fines, turning rebellion into a marketing masterstroke. The "Banned" campaign framed the shoes as the ultimate symbol of rebellion and individuality, cementing Nike's reputation as a brand for champions and rule-breakers.

Phil Knight exemplifies the Executive DRIVE—relentless, strategic, and results-obsessed. But that kind of success doesn't come without pressure. For Executives, the cost of winning is constant: they never stop outperforming the competition, outpacing expectations, and outlasting everyone else.

Executives don't wait for the right moment—they build the plan, lead the charge, and execute with precision. And when they do, they don't just win the game—they redefine it.

Let's take a closer look at the challenges Executives face—and the strengths that make them unstoppable.

Weaknesses of Executives:

- **Impatience with Inefficiency:** Executives expect results and productivity, and they struggle with slow processes and indecision.

- **Relentless Drive Can Lead to Burnout:** Their never-settle mentality can push them to overwork, sometimes at the expense of their health and personal relationships.

- **Control-Oriented:** They prefer to be in charge and may struggle with delegating tasks, believing they can do things better or faster themselves.

- **High Expectations of Others:** They hold themselves to extremely high standards and expect the same from all of those around them, which can create tension if others don't match their level of intensity.

- **Results Over Relationships:** In their pursuit of winning and achieving, they may sometimes overlook the emotional needs of their team or personal connections.

- **Struggle with Adaptability:** Executives thrive in structured, goal-oriented environments but may resist changes that feel unproven or unnecessary.

Strengths of Executives:

- **Driven and Goal-Oriented:** Executives are highly motivated by achievement, setting ambitious targets and relentlessly pursuing success.

- **Decisive and Strategic:** They think fast, act quickly, and make bold decisions, allowing them to seize opportunities and stay ahead.

- **Strong Leadership Presence:** Their confidence, authority, and problem-solving skills make them natural leaders who inspire teams and organizations.

- **Resilient Under Pressure:** Executives thrive in high-stakes situations, remaining calm, focused, and determined despite all obstacles.

- **Highly Competitive:** They love to win and will work tirelessly to stay on top, whether in business, sports, or personal challenges.

- **Efficient and Results-Focused:** Their no-nonsense approach ensures that they streamline processes, eliminate waste, and drive success.

Selling to Executives: Speak in Results

Executives don't buy hopes and promises—they buy results. Every decision they make is driven by achievement, efficiency, and control. If your solution helps them win, streamline operations, or increase profitability, you have their attention. If it wastes their time, you've already lost them.

Skip the fluff. Executives want facts, outcomes, and proof of success. Show them how your product or service delivers measurable results, enhances their competitive edge, or makes them more effective. Be clear, be direct, and don't overcomplicate your pitch. They prefer concise strategies over stories.

Confidence matters. Executives respect competence, decisiveness, and expertise. If you're unsure of your value, they won't trust it, either. Demonstrate efficiency, profitability, or

strategic advantage, and they'll take you seriously. Respect their time, show your knowledge, and position yourself as a trusted resource, not just another salesperson.

Ultimately, Executives make decisions based on logic, efficiency, and impact. Align with their goal-driven mindset, and you won't just close a deal—you'll build a long-term partnership based on performance and results.

If this is your first time reading about your Primary DRIVE, skip the other four and jump straight to Chapter 5 (pg. 77). Once you've finished the book, come back and explore the other DRIVEs to better understand how they impact your customers, clients, and teams. For now, let's see how DRIVE shows up when millions of dollars—and egos—are on the line.

DRIVE in Sales—*Shark Tank*: The Ultimate Test of Sales and Strategy

You are so full of it! There's no chance on God's green earth that this deal could ever possibly close because you would be an idiot among your friends to value this company at $1.5 million or $3 million. It just doesn't add up."

That wasn't some random internet troll. It was billionaire Mark Cuban tearing apart an entrepreneur's valuation on *Shark Tank*, ABC's hit business reality television show that has run for over fifteen seasons. Welcome to the real world of sales, where delusion gets crushed, numbers don't lie, and weak pitches don't stand a chance.

Every episode proves one thing: Not every pitch is created equal. Some entrepreneurs own the room, turning the Sharks against each other. Others get ripped apart before they even finish their pitch. But why?

The right product. The right pitch. The right buyer.

Sales isn't just about having something great—it's about selling that greatness to the correct person in the proper way. Ever watched a pitch and knew immediately which Shark was the perfect fit? Some deals die the second they start—not because the idea is bad, but because it's in front of the wrong Shark.

That's exactly what DRIVE is about: understanding your buyer's psychology and speaking their language.

Watch closely, and you'll see it. Each Shark evaluates deals through their own DRIVE. Some attack with aggressive offers. Others sit back and wait for the right moment. Some demand data. Others look for branding, influence, or raw market potential.

The entrepreneurs who crush it on Shark Tank don't just pitch—they are aware of who their perfect buyer is. And that's where DRIVE gives you the edge in your own sales.

Every Shark Has a DRIVE— And Once You See It, You Can't Unsee It

If you think *Shark Tank* is just about business deals, you're missing the real game. What's actually happening in that tank is pure DRIVE in action—five multimillionaire (or billionaire) investors making decisions based on their deepest buying motivations.

Each Shark has a distinct DRIVE.

- **Director—Robert Herjavec** (*The risk-taker. The thrill-seeker. He invests in passion, vision, and momentum.*)

- **Relator—Lori Greiner** (*The emotional connector. She sees how a product fits into people's lives and relationships.*)

- **Intellectual—Daymond John** (*The strategist. The data-driven investor who looks for proven systems before making a move.*)

- **Validator—Mark Cuban** (*The bold, outspoken investor who backs high-impact ideas and driven entrepreneurs, using his influence to shape industries.*)
- **Executive—Kevin O'Leary** (*The hard-nosed businessman who cares about one thing: winning.*)

Fair warning: after this next section, you won't watch *Shark Tank* the same way again. You'll see DRIVE everywhere—not just in the tank, but in business, sales, and everyday interactions.

Here's the upside: once you can read DRIVE, you have the ultimate edge. You'll know how to connect, influence, and close deals by speaking directly to what drives people to say yes.

Now, let's break down each Shark and how their DRIVE shapes every decision they make.

Robert Herjavec: The Director Who Invests in Freedom

Robert Herjavec isn't just looking for ROI—he's looking for adventure. He invests in lifestyle, freedom, and experiences. If it's fast, exciting, or pushes boundaries, he's in. From kayaks to electric bikes, his deals reflect his Director DRIVE: passion first, numbers second.

Take entrepreneur Jason Woods. In season 3, he pitched Kymera, a jet-propelled bodyboard. It was a disaster. Mark Cuban (Validator) dismissed him as a "want-trepreneur" for failing to launch in ten years. Daymond John (Intellectual) didn't hold back: "This is the worst pitch I have ever seen."

Seven years later, however, Woods came back. This time, he had a finished product and $900,000 in unfulfilled orders. He asked for $250,000 for five percent equity. The Sharks took notice.

Kevin O'Leary (Executive) made a classic power play: $250,000 for five percent, plus a $500 per-unit royalty until he recouped $750,000. Daymond John (Intellectual) countered with $250,000 for ten percent, leveraging his expertise in manufacturing. Mark Cuban (Validator) and Lori Greiner (Relator) passed.

Then Robert Herjavec stepped in.

"I love the product. I love this kind of cool, funky, go-fast stuff . . . I love the second chances. That's what makes this country great: everyone deserves a second chance. I know this space; I think you need more money. I will give you $500,000 for ten percent."

Woods jumped on the offer. His team knew instantly that Robert was the right partner.

Why? Because Woods is also a Director. He spent seventeen years fighting for his vision, quitting his job, raising money, and refusing to quit. Directors don't back down—they double down.

Ironically, Robert overpaid. Woods likely would have taken Daymond's deal at the same percentage. But as a Director, Robert didn't just want the deal—he wanted the ride.

Lori Greiner:
The Relator Who Invests in People

Lori Greiner doesn't just invest in products—she invests in people. While other Sharks chase profit margins, patents, or industry domination, Lori looks for entrepreneurs who care most about their customers. Her top deals aren't built on cutting-edge tech but on real-world solutions that improve lives—from baby gear to personal care to all-natural cleaning products.

Her DRIVE was on full display in season 4, when Ginelle Mills pitched Cool Wazoo, a five-in-one baby product that converted from a changing mat into a shopping cart seat protector. She asked for $65,000 for twenty-five percent equity—but with only $20,000 in sales over a year, the Sharks weren't impressed.

One by one, they dropped out. Even Lori declined. But unlike the others, she offered encouragement, not just criticism.

That's when Mills broke down.

"I have worked so hard," she said through tears. "I am up at 4 a.m., working entrepreneur hours. I underestimated the time it would take. I did not know it was going to be this hard. It took me two years just to design it and source materials."

Lori couldn't ignore Mills' vulnerable confession.

"Ginelle, I am going to come back in. I really like you and I really believe in you. I can see you are going to put your heart and soul into this. I will give you the $65,000 for twenty-five percent."

Kevin O'Leary (Executive) was stunned. "Wow! I would have asked for fifty percent."

But Lori wasn't thinking like an Executive. She wasn't negotiating—she was believing. She didn't invest because she loved the product. She invested because she believed in Mills.

That's what Relators do.

Daymond John:
The Intellectual Who Invests in Systems

One Shark is always the first to ask, "Is it patented?" "Where is it manufactured?" "Tell me about your distribution system." That Shark is Daymond John.

While others get caught up in hype or emotion, Daymond zeroes in on logistics, patents, supply chains, and scalability. He doesn't just invest in products—he invests in systems. His top deals? Manufacturing-heavy businesses like motorcycle helmets, patented insoles, and racing drones. If it needs production, distribution, and supply chain expertise, Daymond is the Shark who makes it happen.

That makes him a clear Intellectual.

In season 6, Patrick Whaley pitched TITIN, a line of weighted compression gear, asking for $500,000 for five percent equity. His biggest struggle? Inventory management and manufacturing.

The final offers came down to:

- Kevin O'Leary (Executive): $500,000 for fifteen percent.
- Daymond John (Intellectual): $500,000 for twenty percent.

Whaley chose Daymond's offer despite the higher equity ask. Why? Because he knew Daymond's expertise in manufacturing and distribution was worth more than the extra five percent.

This is the hidden truth of sales: price isn't always the deciding factor. The best deals happen when the offer aligns with the buyer's DRIVE. TITIN wasn't just looking for funding—it needed an expert to solve its biggest problem.

And that's what Intellectuals do—they don't just invest in ideas. They engineer the systems that make them work.

Mark Cuban:
The Validator Who Invests on Admiration

Mark Cuban chooses to invest in people he trusts and admires. Validators recognize drive, determination, and resilience, and when they see it, they back it all the way.

That's exactly what happened in season 5, when eighteen-year-old Lani Lazzari stepped into the tank with her homemade skincare line, Simple Sugars.

Lani wasn't some polished executive with a team of advisors. She was just eleven years old, struggling with severe eczema, when she decided to create her own solution. What started as a personal fix quickly became something bigger. But turning it into a company? That took years of persistence, resilience, and grit.

The Sharks, however, weren't impressed. One by one, they passed.

Lori Greiner (Relator) didn't see a strong retail angle. Robert Herjavec (Director) didn't feel the excitement. Daymond John (Intellectual) questioned its scalability.

Then Kevin O'Leary (Executive) took aim. "This is the most competitive industry on Earth. There's nothing proprietary about what you're doing. It's so simple that even an eleven-year-old can do it." He didn't stop there. He told her outright that her company wasn't worth a million dollars—and never would be.

Most entrepreneurs would have crumbled, but young Lani stood firm. She knew her numbers. She knew her product. She knew her customers. Cuban saw it immediately. "You remind me of me when I was getting started." He didn't see just a skincare company. He saw a fighter. Someone who had spent years grinding to build something real. Someone who wouldn't quit, no matter how tough things got. "I like investing in people who have overcome challenges." He offered her $100,000 for 33% equity. She took the deal.

In just six weeks, Simple Sugars hit $1 million in sales.

This is how Validators operate. They don't just chase numbers— they bet on grit, hunger, and the will to win. Because when a Validator believes in you? They don't just invest—they elevate you.

Kevin O'Leary:
The Executive Who Invests in Proof

Kevin O'Leary doesn't gamble. He doesn't invest in hype, hope, or "potential." He invests in proof found in cold, hard numbers.

That's exactly why Donna and Rosy Khalife walked away empty-handed when they pitched Surprise Ride in season 5 of *Shark Tank*. Their kids' craft kit subscription service had a compelling story— 220 subscribers and projected $500,000 in sales for the next year. They asked for $110,000 for 10% equity, valuing their company at $1.1 million.

The Sharks weren't buying it. Kevin didn't even make an offer. The numbers weren't strong enough. Robert Herjavec (Director) saw potential and offered $110,000 for 25%, but the Khalife sisters hesitated and walked away without a deal.

Over the next few years, Surprise Ride's business exploded, hitting over $1 million in annual sales and turning profitable. The Khalife sisters proved they could execute, adapt, and win.

And that's when Kevin O'Leary took notice. In 2016, during a *Beyond the Tank* follow-up episode, Kevin saw what he had been waiting for—proof. The Khalife sisters had built a thriving, profitable business, and now it was worth his investment. This time, he was ready to make a deal. "$50,000 for 2.5% equity, plus a 6% royalty until I recoup $150,000." The Khalifes didn't hesitate. They took the deal.

Kevin grinned. "Now I own a piece of this company . . . and I'm going to pour gasoline on this fire to get it to $10 million in sales."

This moment made *Shark Tank* history—the first time a Shark returned to invest in a company they originally passed on. Why? Because Executives don't bet on maybes—they bet on certainties. Kevin O'Leary doesn't chase potential. He waits. He watches. He invests when success is inevitable. And when an Executive finally puts their money in? They make sure it multiplies.

The 20/80 Rule in Action: Shark Tank's Buying Patterns

The 20/80 Rule isn't just theory—it plays out in every sales conversation, including *Shark Tank*. Each shark evaluates deals through their DRIVE, instinctively favoring pitches that align with their unique buying motivations. This is why some Sharks close more deals than others—not because they're better investors, but because certain pitches speak directly to their DRIVE.

Shark Tank Closing Stats

Name	Times Pitched	Deals Closed	Closing Ratio
Robert Herjavec (Director)	511	57	11%
Lori Greiner (Relator)	311	61	19%
Daymond John (Intellectual)	407	61	15%
Mark Cuban (Validator)	403	85	19%
Kevin O'Leary (Executive)	531	40	8%

Look closely at the numbers:

- Lori Greiner (Relator) and Mark Cuban (Validator) close the most deals. Why? Relators invest in people, and Validators invest in strong, credible opportunities. If an entrepreneur earns their trust, respect, and proves their expertise, they'll jump in.

- Kevin O'Leary (Executive) has the lowest close rate. Why? Because Executives only invest in sure things. If the numbers don't prove it, they don't buy.

- Daymond John (Intellectual) closes deals when the pitch makes sense. If the entrepreneur clearly explains the strategy and long-term plan, he's in. If it's hype without substance, he's out.

- Robert Herjavec (Director) has a lower-than-average close rate. Why? Because Directors need to feel inspired by a pitch. If it doesn't excite them, they're out.

People Don't Just Buy— They Buy Based on Their DRIVE

Think about the last time you made a big decision, whether it was a purchase, an investment, or even a major life move. Was it purely logical? Or did it come down to something deeper and more personal?

We like to believe we make rational, calculated choices. But the truth?

People put their money where their DRIVE is.

In business and sales, you often hear the phrase, "Put your money where your mouth is." But in reality, people purchase based on what supports their DRIVE.

Look at the largest investments each Shark has ever made. Each one is a direct reflection of their DRIVE.

That's why Robert Herjavec (Director) isn't looking for spreadsheets and market trends—he's looking for revolution. When Zero Pollution Motors pitched cars that run on compressed air, he saw more than a company. He saw the future. He dropped $5 million into the deal—not because of cold, hard facts, but because Directors don't buy into what exists. They buy into what's possible.

Lori Greiner (Relator) doesn't care about disruptive technology—she cares about people. When she saw RuffleButts, a children's clothing brand, she didn't just see profits. She saw parents. She saw families. She saw a product that brought value to the people who needed it most. That's why she invested $600,000, because Relators buy into relationships.

Daymond John (Intellectual) doesn't get caught up in hype—he bets on systems, patents, and logistics. That's why Hells Bells Helmets got his $500,000 investment. It wasn't just a product—it was manufacturing, safety regulations, and a distribution model that made sense. Intellectuals don't chase fads. They buy into structured, scalable success.

Mark Cuban (Validator) isn't just looking for the next big thing—he's looking for entrepreneurs who can change the game. When he invested $2 million in Ten Thirty One Productions, it wasn't just about numbers. It was about impact. Validators buy into businesses that leave a mark, reshape industries, and elevate those behind them. Cuban buys into the people who have what it takes to build empires.

And then there's Kevin O'Leary (Executive). He doesn't buy into dreams. He buys into proof. That's why Zipz, a patented single-serve wine company, landed his $2.5 million investment. Because Executives are the ones who back certainties, high margins, proven demand, and scalability. That's what an Executive looks for, and that's why Zipz got the deal.

The largest purchases the Sharks made? They weren't just big bets—they were perfectly aligned with their DRIVE.

This is the hidden side of sales. It's not just about numbers, discounts, or ROI. It's about understanding what truly moves the buyer. Because when you understand why someone buys, you understand how to sell to them. And then everything changes.

The Perfect Pitch: Selling All the Sharks

Every salesperson dreams of the perfect pitch—the kind that doesn't just get an offer but creates a feeding frenzy where buyers start fighting over who gets to work with you.

Most entrepreneurs on *Shark Tank* struggle just to land one investor. But during season 5, episode 2, Charles Michael Yim made history by achieving the impossible. He didn't just convince a shark to invest—he got all five. Instead of competing against him, the Sharks started competing against each other to be part of his business.

How?

Because he didn't just pitch a product. Yim walked into the Tank seeking $250,000 for 10% of Breathometer, his smartphone-compatible breathalyzer. Without knowing DRIVE, he instinctively tailored his pitch to match what motivated each shark to buy.

- Robert Herjavec (Director): Yim led with innovation, speed, and disruption, framing Breathometer as a game-changer in tech. Directors buy into big, bold ideas that shake up the future and Robert was hooked.

- Lori Greiner (Relator): He pivoted to safety, responsibility, and personal well-being. Lori isn't driven by tech—she's driven by how products help people. Once she saw how Breathometer could save lives, she was in.

- Daymond John (Intellectual): Next, Yim broke down the science, logistics, and manufacturing strategy. Intellectuals don't buy based on emotion—they want facts, data, and scalable systems. Once Daymond saw the structure behind it, he backed the deal.

- Mark Cuban (Validator): Yim framed Breathometer as an industry disruptor—something game-changing. Validators want to champion revolutionary ideas, and the chance to be part of a category-defining product made Cuban take the leap.

- Kevin O'Leary (**Executive**): Finally, Yim sealed the deal with undeniable proof—hard numbers, clear financials, and market validation. Kevin doesn't invest in dreams. He invests in certainties. The numbers were too strong to ignore.

The Feeding Frenzy

It was chaos in the tank. Instead of negotiating with Yim, the Sharks turned on each other, trying to structure the best deal. Offers flew. Counteroffers escalated. The energy in the room shifted from skepticism to excitement, from doubt to urgency.

The Sharks were no longer in control. Yim was. They wanted in so badly, they kicked him out of the tank to battle it out behind closed doors.

Think about that.

An entrepreneur walked into the tank hoping to convince one Shark to invest—and walked out while the Sharks battled over who got to write the check.

When the dust settled, Yim didn't just get his $250,000. The Sharks offered him $1,000,000. A 400% increase. And his company valuation? It skyrocketed from $2.5 million to $3.3 million.

Not because he had the best product.

Not because he had the best margins.

Because he pitched to every single buyer's DRIVE.

Why This Changes Everything for Sales

This wasn't luck. It wasn't magic.

Yim did exactly what the best salespeople do every day. He understood that selling isn't about pushing a product—it's about speaking to what truly motivates the buyer.

Most salespeople give the same pitch to every buyer. The best? They speak directly to their DRIVE—and close deals others never could.

If Charles Michael Yim could walk into the tank and turn the Sharks against each other just by instinctively matching his pitch to their buying behaviors, imagine what you could do if you knew your client's DRIVE with absolute precision. This is the raw power of understanding what *actually* moves people to buy—not just in a high-stakes boardroom, but in every sales conversation, pitch, and negotiation you'll ever experience.

Soon, you'll walk into any room, *own* the conversation, and close deals others never even see coming. This is the 20/80 rule in action: master the other four buying languages, and you have the potential to increase your sales reach by 400%—turning lost opportunities into closed deals.

Now that you see how DRIVE shapes every buying decision, the only question left is—how do you use it to close more deals, crush the competition, and dominate in sales?

Welcome to the DRIVE Sales System. Let's get to work.

6

DRIVE Sales System Overview

The pickaxe shattered the rocks. The tunnel was dark and cold. The only light came from the flickering flame of oil lanterns, casting long shadows over a lonely man chasing his dream. R.U. Darby's uncle— a man gripped by "gold fever" in the early days of the Colorado gold rush—wasn't a prospector by trade. He wasn't a miner. He was just a man with a belief that somewhere beneath his boots, the earth held the fortune that would change his life. So he staked a claim, grabbed a shovel, and started digging.

The work was brutal. Each swing of the pickaxe echoed through the narrow shaft like a shot in the dark. But he kept going. He kept showing up. Day after day, he dug deeper. And then—pay dirt. He struck gold. Real gold. A shimmering, substantial vein that promised wealth beyond imagination.

There was only one problem: he didn't have the machinery to pull it out.

So he covered the entrance to the mine, headed back home to Williamsburg, Maryland, and told his nephew, R.U. Darby, what he'd found. Together, they raised money from friends and neighbors, bought the necessary equipment, and hauled it across the country. When they returned to Colorado, the air buzzed with certainty. The first load of ore was sent off to the smelter—and the results were staggering. This wasn't a fluke. They were sitting on one of the richest veins in the region. A few more shipments and they'd be debt-free. After that? All profit.

They were already mentally spending their future profits. Then, all of a sudden, the gold just disappeared. The drills went down. The tension went up. They pushed deeper, harder, trying to relocate the vein. But the walls stayed silent. The earth gave nothing back. After weeks of coming up empty, they did what most people do when they meet resistance: they quit.

The two men sold everything—machinery, tools, the claim itself—to a local junk man for a few hundred bucks, and caught the next train east. Completely and utterly defeated.

But that junk man wasn't interested in the scrap. He had a few key things the Darbys didn't: a system, a strategy, and a professional who knew where to look. He brought in a mining engineer, someone who understood fault lines and rock formations. The engineer ran calculations, studied the terrain, and came back with a simple insight: the previous owners had quit just three feet from the vein. Just three feet.

The junk man drilled exactly where the engineer told him to and hit gold. He pulled millions from the very place Darby and his uncle had abandoned.

Three feet. Stopping just three feet short had cost them everything.

It sounds unbelievable until you realize salespeople do the exact same thing every day. They quit too soon. They pitch the wrong way. They chase leads without a plan, hoping repetition will do what clarity never could. Not because they're lazy but because they don't have a system.

The DRIVE Sales System is that system. It's how you stop guessing and grinding and start connecting with people the way they're wired to buy. It doesn't just help you find the gold—it shows you where to strike again and again even when you find resistance.

Because the truth is this: You don't rise to the level of your expectations—you fall to the level of your training. That insight was first spoken in 645 BC by the Greek poet Archilochus, and nearly 2,700 years later, it still holds true. Modern author James Clear echoed the same principle in *Atomic Habits* when he wrote, "We don't rise to the level of our goals. We fall to the level of our systems."

Hope is not a strategy and hustle is not a plan. You need a system, one that works with people, not against them. One that turns your pitch into a perfect match for their motivation.

The **S.A.L.E.S.** system gives you that blueprint, step-by-step:

- **S—Start with Their D.R.I.V.E.**
  Understand what emotionally drives their decisions.

- **A—Assess Their Needs**
  Ask S.U.P.E.R. questions to uncover what matters most—so you spend less time guessing and more time getting to the heart of their motivation.

- **L—Leverage Your Solutions**
  Present your offer in a way that aligns with their motivation.

- **E—Eliminate Their Concerns**
  Handle objections through emotional and logical clarity.

- **S—Sell Them Their D.R.I.V.E. Solution**
  Tailor your close to their Primary and Secondary DRIVE.

Each chapter that follows gives you the exact moves to master every detail and nuance of this system so you can stop losing deals that should've been yours. When you understand D.R.I.V.E. and follow the S.A.L.E.S. framework, you don't just get better at selling—you become the kind of salesperson people never forget.

One who connects faster. Closes stronger. And wins more consistently.

This is your edge. Let's sharpen it.

7

S—Start with Their DRIVE

With a seven-figure contract on the line, Jerry* received the kind of call most people only dream of. Fred Smith—the legendary founder and CEO of FedEx—was ready to talk. This wasn't just any meeting. Jerry's company specialized in high-level strategic consulting for Fortune 100 companies. These proposals usually took months—sometimes even years—of groundwork before they reached the decision-maker's office. And now, Fred Smith's personal assistant was inviting Jerry to FedEx headquarters in Memphis, Tennessee. This wasn't just a door opening—it was the vault swinging wide.

Jerry cleared his schedule, booked a same-day flight, and left everything behind to prepare for this once-in-a-lifetime shot. When he arrived at the sprawling, fortress-like FedEx campus, he was buzzing with anticipation. This was it—the meeting that could change the trajectory of his entire company. He was escorted to the executive lobby, offered a bottle of water, and told that Mr. Smith would be informed of his arrival.

But then, everything drastically shifted. A sharply dressed assistant walked briskly across the lobby, holding something in her hand. It was Jerry's original proposal, still sealed. On top of it was a bright yellow sticky note with just three brutal words: *"Know Your Customer."*

That was it. No handshake. No meeting. No second chance.

Jerry's heart sank. He knew exactly what had gone wrong. One of his team members—likely without thinking—had overnighted the proposal in a UPS envelope . . . to the FedEx building. Fred Smith certainly didn't open it. Why would he? The proposal had arrived in the hands of his greatest competitor. To Smith, it wasn't just a tone-deaf mistake—it was disrespectful. There would be no conversation. No contract. No recovery. The meeting was over before it began.

When Jerry told me that story, my stomach dropped. I asked him, "What did you do?"

He looked me dead in the eye and replied, "I got back on the plane and went home—with the most expensive business lesson of my life echoing in my head: *Know. Your. Customer.*"

Let that sink in for a moment.

Jerry didn't lose the deal because of a weak pitch, a pricing issue, or the wrong strategy. He lost it because someone on his team didn't understand the golden rule of business: Everything has to be about your customer. It has to be about their world view. Their values. Their language. In essence, it has to be about their DRIVE.

This is where it all begins. Every person you sell to has two DRIVEs steering their decisions: one emotional, one logical.

The Primary DRIVE is their emotional GPS—the "why" behind their choices. It's what lights them up inside. For some, it's the pursuit of freedom. For others, it's connection, understanding, recognition, or control. This is the moment that makes them lean in, feel seen, and think, *Yes, this is for me.*

But they also have a Secondary DRIVE: the logic filter. It's "how" they justify the decision. It asks, *Does this make sense? Can I explain this to myself or others?* And here's the truth: when you speak both languages—emotion and logic—you don't just make a sale. You create raving fans. People who buy in, buy again, and bring others with them.

Pro Tip: As you go through this system, be prepared to make some mental notes—or better yet, write down your client's Primary and Secondary DRIVE. You'll be using both in every step that follows. You sell to the Primary. You close to their Secondary.

That's why, in the DRIVE S.A.L.E.S. System, the very first S stands for Start with Their DRIVE. Because if you don't start with them, you may never get the chance to finish.

There's more than one way to unlock someone's DRIVE—and in sales, just like in life, context is everything. You don't hand someone a full assessment the moment you've shaken their hand for the first time, and you definitely don't dive into deep psychology while standing in line at a conference buffet.

Different moments call for different tools. You've got to know which one to use and when to use it. That's why this material is broken down into three levels: Good, Better, and Best. Each one is powerful in its own right. Each one has a purpose. But if you want to dominate in sales—or leadership, parenting, relationships, or business—you've got to master all three.

- **GOOD:** *The Conversation Close.*
  This is your go-to when the interaction is quick, casual, or unexpected—like meeting someone at a networking event, talking on the phone, or making a first impression. It's light, fast, and deceptively effective. It allows you to get *just enough* information to pivot your approach and speak to what matters to them.

- **BETTER:** *The DRIVE Sales Cards.*
  This is where things get real. When you're sitting across the table from someone who knows why they're there—to explore working together—this method lets you go deeper. The cards give you an instant read on their buying language. In under five minutes, you'll know what drives them—and exactly how to sell to them.

- **BEST:** *The 35-Question Online DRIVE Assessment.*
  This is for the serious ones. The ones who are ready to go deeper—whether they're a client, a friend, or a teammate. This tool isn't just about closing a deal. It's about building a long-term

relationship based on trust, alignment, and service. And best of all? It's deadly accurate. This is how you discover someone's true DRIVE with precision and use it to serve them better than anyone else ever has.

Each of these methods has a place in your arsenal. Master them, and you'll stop guessing what motivates people and start selling directly to what matters.

Good: The Conversation Close

There are two things you should never say when you're meeting someone for the first time:

1. "Are you married?"
2. "What do you do for a living?"

Let me tell you why.

That first question—"Are you married?"—might sound harmless, even friendly. But statistically speaking, nearly 50% of people have been divorced. So there's a good chance that casual question just triggered a landmine of resentment, heartbreak, or legal drama. Now? They're associating you with the pain of their past.

And the second one—"What do you do?"—is even worse. According to a Gallup poll, over 70% of people are unhappy in their job. So when you lead with that question, you just dragged them into the very thing they're trying to escape from—right in the middle of a moment that was supposed to be about possibility, excitement, or building something new. Instead of earning trust, you triggered stress. Instead of making a connection, you made them feel stuck.

Let's be real: Those two questions are generic and lazy. And if you want to master the art of connection—real connection—you have to go deeper. You have to speak to something more meaningful than their LinkedIn headline or relationship status.

That's where *The Conversation Close* comes in.

This isn't a gimmick. This is how you tap into the real person sitting across from you—without needing cards, a form, or a full-blown assessment. You can use it at a networking event, on a Zoom call, or in a random hallway conversation. It's quick, clean, and when done right, it can lead to big results.

Keith Cardinal spent years as a supply chain consultant for billion-dollar companies like SpaceX, Microsoft, and Google. When he hit his fifties, he knew it was time for a shift. He wanted more purpose. More freedom. So he left it all behind and stepped into business consulting—with zero clients and zero leads. But within his first month, Keith used *The Conversation Close* and landed over $25,000 in commission—just from one simple chat that led to a real connection. No pitch. No slide deck. Just three simple questions that mattered.

Here are the three *Conversation Close* questions that can change everything:

1. Other than work and family, what are you most passionate about?

2. When you don't get to do (insert passion), how does it impact you?

3. When you do get to do (insert passion), how does it make you feel?

These questions are deceptively simple. But pay close attention to how people respond because inside their answers are clues to their DRIVE.

- If they light up talking about travel, creativity, freedom, adventure, and overcoming challenges—they're a **Director.**

- If they share about their family, friendships, faith, or serving their community—they're a **Relator.**

- If they mention reading, organizing, healthy habits, being in nature, or personal growth—they're an **Intellectual.**

- If they describe wanting to be seen, respected, valued, or praised—they're a **Validator.**

- If they talk about winning, building, achieving, solving, or providing—they're an **Executive.**

You don't need a psychological profile to spot someone's DRIVE. You just need to listen differently—and ask the kind of questions that cut through the noise. This is how you connect. This is how you build trust. This is how you open the door to influence, impact, and income, without ever sounding like a salesperson.

Master *The Conversation Close*, and you'll never walk into a room and feel powerless again because you'll know how to speak to what matters most.

Test Your DRIVE Radar

Can you read between the lines? You've learned the power of *The Conversation Close*. Now it's time to test your instincts. Below are six real client responses—people I've worked with directly—who answered the three Conversation Close questions. Your job? Read their answers and try to identify their Primary DRIVE. Don't overthink it. Go with your gut. This exercise isn't about being perfect—it's about sharpening your ability to listen for motivation beneath their spoken words.

Before you start, here's a quick refresher on what each DRIVE really wants:

- **Director** = Lifestyle (Freedom, Experience, Challenge, Creativity)
- **Relator** = Community (Connection, Family, Service, Faith)
- **Intellectual** = Systems (Learning, Health, Nature, Efficiency)
- **Validator** = Admiration (Respect, Recognition, Trust, Personal Praise)
- **Executive** = Proof (Achievement, Winning, Control, Security)

Let's sharpen your DRIVE skills by experiencing them.

Client #1: Leesa Clark-Price—CEO of Warrior Princess

Q: Other than work and family, what are you most passionate about?

A: Empowering other people, especially women.

Q: When you don't get to empower women, how does it impact you?

A: I don't feel important, I feel like I've lost purpose and meaning.

Q: When you do empower women, how does it make you feel?

A: Incredibly blessed to have a positive impact in others' lives.

Client #2: Richard Stock—Real Estate Investor

Q: Other than work and family, what are you most passionate about?

A: Traveling.

Q: When you don't get to travel, how does it impact you?

A: I feel like I'm failing, like I can't accomplish all I want. I feel like I'm letting others down.

Q: When you travel, how does it make you feel?

A: I love experiencing new things and cultures. I feel free and accomplished.

Client #3: Eric Counts—Professional Speaker / Credit Repair Specialist

Q: Other than work and family, what are you most passionate about?

A: Work.

Q: When you don't get to work, how does it impact you?

A: Very negatively. I feel like I'm letting a lot of people down.

Q: When you do work, how do you feel?

A: I feel validated. What I do gives me recognition and trust from my audience.

Client #4: Justin Prince—Entrepreneur With Over $2 Billion in Revenue

Q: Other than work and family, what are you most passionate about?

A: Serving and inspiring people.

Q: When you don't get to serve/inspire, how does it impact you?

A: I feel out of alignment, disenchanted—like I've let people down.

Q: When you do serve/inspire, how do you feel?

A: Like I'm doing what I was put on Earth to do. Full. Purposeful.

Client #5: Christian George—Entrepreneur / Investor / Educator

Q: Other than work and family, what are you most passionate about?

A: Learning, creating systems, contributing.

Q: When you don't learn something new, how does it impact you?

A: It stifles me. I feel inefficient and frustrated.

Q: When you do learn, how do you feel?

A: Energized. I gain time, get more done, and feel like I'm growing.

Client #6: Daniela Camacho—Corporate Manager

Q: Other than work and family, what are you most passionate about?

A: Working and putting money in the bank.

Q: When you don't work/save, how does it impact you?

A: I feel stressed and incompetent.

Q: When you do work/save, how do you feel?

A: At peace. Safe.

Based on their answers, assign the Primary DRIVE to each of these six people. Circle back when you're ready to check your answers.

Answer Key:

Leesa Price—Relator (Her passion is empowering others and finding purpose in service)

Richard Stock—Director (Craves freedom, experience, and personal challenge)

Eric Counts—Validator (Clear emphasis on recognition, trust, and personal praise)

Justin Prince—Relator (Deep sense of calling to serve and impact others)

Christian George—Intellectual (Learning, growth, systems, and internal efficiency)

Daniela Camacho—Executive (Security, work ethic, and results-driven mindset)

Pro Tip: When in Doubt, Tie It Back to Their Passion

If you're ever unsure about someone's DRIVE after a first conversation, don't freeze. Just tie their passion back to how your product or service creates value for them. Every passion has a doorway to a DRIVE. You just have to be creative enough to find it.

- **Selling to Leesa (Relator)?** Talk about how your product *empowers women* and helps her *serve her community*.

- **Selling to Richard (Director)?** Show how it gives him more *freedom to travel, explore, and feel alive*.

- **Selling to Eric (Validator)?** Position it as a way to *stand out, get recognized, and build trust* with his audience.

- **Selling to Justin (Relator)?** Frame your solution as a platform for *impact, purpose, and service to others*.

- **Selling to Christian (Intellectual)?** Highlight how your product helps him *learn faster, create better systems, or optimize his time*.

- **Selling to Daniela (Executive)?** Prove how it helps her *win, save, achieve, or protect what she's working so hard to build*.

And remember: Once the door is open, you've earned the right to go deeper. Use the DRIVE Cards or the Full Assessment to get surgical with your message. But when time is short? *The Conversation Close* is your sharpest tool.

Listen to what makes them light up—and speak straight to it.

Better: DRIVE Cards

"I just made $50,000 in 24 hours using DRIVE. Want me to show you how I did it?"

That was the text that changed my world—and maybe yours, too.

It didn't come from a sales guru. It didn't come from a bestselling author. It came from Mitch Nelson—a rookie in his company trying to find his edge. That one bold message launched him to the top of his sales leaderboard, and eventually, the top income earner in the entire company of over 2000 salespeople.

The moment I saw his message, I called him on the spot because I had to know what he'd done. What he shared was nothing short of brilliant.

I had created DRIVE to help people understand themselves—to figure out what fuels them internally. Mitch flipped the script. He used DRIVE to decode *other people*. And by doing so, he closed $50,000 in sales in a single day.

He took the seven identity words from each DRIVE—words that make people feel important—and wrote them on 3×5 cards.

Then he laid those cards in front of his clients and said:

"I want to get to know you better. This simple DRIVE personality profile will help me serve you more effectively. Read these cards, then rank them based on what makes you *feel* important—not what's important to you."

No pressure. No manipulation. Just insight. Once the cards were ranked, Mitch had the keys to their buyer's code. He knew exactly how to speak their language. And more importantly, he knew what *not* to say. That moment was the catalyst.

I realized if a new salesperson could use DRIVE to close at that level, anyone could. So I built a full professional DRIVE Card System. In less than five minutes, you'll know what motivates your client. And on the back of every card is a cheat sheet that tells you how to sell to them, speak their language, and even where they prefer to meet.

I wanted to include the cards directly in this book, but manufacturing made that impossible. Instead, you can get your own free set at **DriveSalesCards.com**. You can order a personal set or grab them in bulk for your entire team. The cards are completely free—you just cover a small shipping and handling fee. Get yours while supplies last.

And once you have them, go to **DriveSalesCards.com/Script** for step-by-step instructions on how to implement the cards into your sales presentations, client meetings, or even team building sessions.

Best: Online DRIVE Assessment

The greatest salespeople aren't just exceptional closers. They're powerful connectors. And at the highest level of connection, surface-level shortcuts won't cut it.

That's where the Online DRIVE Assessment comes in.

This is the most accurate, comprehensive, and insightful way to discover someone's DRIVE. It goes beyond casual questions or quick rankings. It's a 35-question assessment designed to uncover what makes someone feel important at the deepest level—personally, professionally, and emotionally.

And here's the best part: you can use it with your team, your spouse, your business partner, or even your kids. It is a unique tool for anyone whose world you want to understand—and influence—with clarity and compassion.

Why This Is the Best

Let's break it down:

- *The Conversation Close* gives you a read in the moment.
- The DRIVE Cards give you a structured shortcut to clarity.
- But the Online DRIVE Assessment gives you a map—one that's been stress-tested, refined, and validated across thousands of real-world applications.

It doesn't just tell you someone's Primary and Secondary DRIVE. It shows you *why* they operate the way they do. What they protect. What they crave. What they will fight for—and what shuts them down. It's the difference between guessing and knowing. Between a sale and a relationship. Between a customer and a client for life.

How to Use It

When the time is right—when trust has been built and you're ready to take the relationship to a deeper level—the next step is simple: invite them to take the full DRIVE Assessment. It's quick, eye-opening, and gives both of you something rare in business: clarity. By understanding their unique combination of motivations, you'll gain the ability to communicate with precision, lead with empathy, and serve in a way that actually resonates. Whether you're working one-on-one or onboarding a new team member, this is the moment where real connection meets strategy.

Get the Assessment

Go to **WhatIsMyDRIVE.com** to take the full Online DRIVE Assessment. This is how you stop speaking *your* language and start selling in *theirs*.

Pro Tip: Stop Guessing. Start Closing.

Ready to turn DRIVE into your unfair advantage? Join our exclusive DRIVE Mastermind & Membership—the go-to system for sales professionals, coaches, and business leaders who are done guessing and ready to close with accuracy. You'll receive your own custom assessment link to send to new prospects, potential clients, and existing team members. The moment they take it, you get real-time results delivered straight to your inbox.

But that's just the beginning.

Membership includes weekly live masterminds, full access to our training vault, entry into our exclusive private community, and the complete 57-page DRIVE Assessment Reports—custom-built to help you speak your client's language, close faster, and build loyalty that lasts. And the real game-changer? Our custom DRIVE+AI platform gives you a DRIVE-trained AI that helps you write emails, craft social posts, develop marketing strategies, and tailor messaging for every DRIVE type.

Go to **DriveSalesMastermind.com** and join now to gain your competitive advantage.

The Power of the Obvious

There's an underlying truth most salespeople never grasp: breakthroughs don't come from complexity—they come from paying attention.

In October 1962, the world stood on the brink of nuclear war. The U.S. and the Soviet Union were locked in a tense standoff over missiles in Cuba. One wrong move, and the entire planet could have gone up in irreparable flames. Inside the Oval Office, pressure was mounting. American generals were pushing for immediate airstrikes. President John F. Kennedy was walking a tightrope between global catastrophe and yet another political disaster.

Then, in the middle of the high-strung chaos, a single CIA analyst walked in with fresh U-2 spy plane photos and said two simple words: "Look closer." Everyone leaned in. The analyst pointed to a small cluster of fields—barely noticeable. "They've built soccer fields," he said.

The generals didn't get it. "So what?" one of them asked.

The analyst didn't flinch. "Cubans don't play soccer. Russians do."

That tiny, overlooked detail changed everything. It confirmed that Soviet troops were already on the ground in Cuba. It turned speculation into certainty. It gave Kennedy the upper hand—and ultimately helped him negotiate a peaceful resolution. World War III was averted . . . because someone noticed what was right in front of them. All they had to do was look closer.

Sales, leadership, and influence all work the same way. People think they need a perfect pitch, a complex CRM strategy, or a 10-step objection-rebuttal matrix. But most of the time, the answers are sitting in plain sight. You just have to pay attention.

I once worked with a branch president at KeyBank who was frustrated because she couldn't figure out how to motivate her team. She wanted insight—but didn't feel comfortable asking her employees directly. To show her how easy it could be, I walked up to one of her tellers. She had a miniature Eiffel Tower on her desk and pictures of herself in various travel destinations. I simply asked, "I love the Eiffel Tower—have you been there?"

Her eyes lit up. "Not yet! But I've been to Greece, Germany, New York, Australia . . . I'm saving up to go to Paris." For the next five minutes, she told me all about her dream of becoming a flight attendant, her honeymoon adventures, and how travel made her feel alive.

When I returned to the branch president, she was stunned by what I discovered. "She's never told me any of that and I've worked with her for over a year."

I smiled back at her. "You never asked."

That teller was a Director—motivated by freedom, adventure, and experience. And all the clues were sitting on her desk the entire time.

Establishing Your Uniqueness

In a noisy, cluttered world, being memorable is your edge. The Good, Better, Best Method and each of its varying elements we've covered will help you stand out, build trust quickly, and create instant credibility. It's not just about what you say—it's about how you make people feel.

And nothing makes someone feel more understood than when you know what drives them.

Observation is the greatest sales skill. Whether you're using *The Conversation Close,* DRIVE Cards, or the full Assessment, your attention is your most powerful tool.

People reveal their DRIVE in how they talk, decorate, behave, and what they protect. The Director will defend their freedom. The Relator will defend their relationships. The Intellectual will defend their logic and learning. The Validator will defend their worth. And the Executive will defend their results.

But once you see their DRIVE, what do you do next? You'll need more than instincts. You'll need questions that cut through surface talk and reveal what truly matters. In the next chapter, we'll master the second step of the DRIVE S.A.L.E.S. System—**Assess Their Needs.** Because the secret to eliminating objections, resistance, and uncertainty . . . is asking the right questions first.

8

A—Assess Their Needs

I need you at the base—NOW! This is the biggest deal we've ever had, and it's falling apart. Everything depends on you!"

Levi McPherson had been with BWI, a satellite technology company, for exactly one week when his CEO screamed those demands into the phone. He had no knowledge of the deal. No time to prepare. In fifteen minutes, he'd be walking into a room full of high-ranking military officers—expecting answers he didn't have.

He sprinted to his car, gripping the phone as the CEO told him he was about to get on a plane but didn't share any other details. All Levi had to go on was a name: the CEO of the joint-venture company. If anyone could offer insight into this contract, it was him. Levi punched the number into his phone. It rang. The call connected.

"I'm going into surgery right now. I won't be able to help. You're on your own. Don't screw it up."

The words landed like a death sentence. Then the call went dead. Levi's stomach clenched. No backup. No plan. Just him. The largest contract in BWI's history was on the line and he was flying blind.

When he arrived at the military base, the secretary's expression was tense. "Hurry, the meeting has already started," she said, her voice clipped with urgency. He wasn't just unprepared—he was late.

Another woman with a razor-sharp expression flung open the door, ushering him into a massive military conference room where twelve highly decorated officers sat in silence. Their faces were unreadable, their eyes locked on Levi as if he had just stepped into hostile territory.

The weight of the moment crashed down on him. He knew two things. First, he had absolutely no idea what these men expected him to discuss in detail. Second, he had to find a way to save this deal. His heart pounded. His mind raced. If he opened his mouth and started talking, he would expose himself in an instant. He couldn't fake knowledge he didn't have. But he could do something else.

Standing at the front of the boardroom, surrounded by skeptical faces and crossed arms, he took a slow breath and steadied his voice. "Gentlemen, I understand there's frustration with this project. What I need to know is—what does success look like to you? If I could wave a magic wand, what would the perfect outcome be?" The air in the room thickened. The officers exchanged glances, their silence stretching into tension. Then, finally, one of them spoke. "We were promised it would be done by October. No updates. No action."

There it was. The real problem.

Levi took a seat, grabbed his pen and legal pad, and started asking questions. They answered. Timeline. Budget. Deliverables. Every critical piece of information was handed to him—because he used a technique we call ASK. Don't Tell. ASK stands for Always Seek Knowledge.

Twenty minutes later, he put his pen down. "It's my job to make this project match your goals," Levi said. "So, if we hit these deadlines and stay on budget, do we have a deal?"

The officers glanced at each other. A few nods began around the table. Then, unanimously, they answered, "Yes."

Levi had just saved the biggest contract in company history—without knowing a single detail about it. He didn't pitch. He didn't fake confidence. He simply **Assessed Their Needs.**

Now, put yourself in that room. Would you have panicked? Would you have tried to bluff your way through? Or would you have done what Levi did—Assess Their Needs and let the buyer tell you exactly how to close them?

Listen to Learn—Don't Assume and Assault

Most salespeople make one critical mistake: they ask just enough questions to give themselves permission to speak. The moment they sense an opening, they dive into an assault of product features, timelines, pricing, and deliverables—assuming their client is ready to hear all of these things. This isn't salesmanship; it's sales ambush. It's like prescribing medication without diagnosing the illness.

Gong.io's data science team analyzed one million B2B sales calls and discovered something remarkable: top-performing sales reps talk only 46% of the time, while bottom-performing reps dominate conversations by talking 72% of the time. The data makes it crystal clear—success in sales isn't about talking more; it's about listening better.

Imagine walking into a doctor's office and, before you've even described your symptoms, the doctor jumps in excitedly and announces: "Today only—25% off colonoscopies! Did you know one in every twenty Americans develops colon cancer? Colonoscopies are your best defense—comprehensive, effective, and thorough. Let's get you scheduled immediately. How's 2:00 p.m. today?"

Bewildered, you respond, "Doctor, thanks, but I'm just here for a flu shot."

Without asking questions first, the doctor has only created confusion and distance between your real needs and the benefits she might have provided. Doctors enjoy an exceptionally high closing ratio precisely because they ASK.

Masterful selling is about listening deeply enough to uncover truths even your prospect didn't fully recognize. When you shift from assumption to genuine curiosity, you transform the sales conversation from interrogation to revelation.

Here's a simple yet profound truth:

- **Spend 90% of your time Assessing Their Needs, and you'll spend only 10% Eliminating Their Concerns.**

- **Spend just 10% Assessing Their Needs, and you're doomed to spend 90% Eliminating Their Concerns.**

The choice is yours—invest in clarity upfront or pay the price later in endless objections and doubt.

In the previous chapter, we anchored your approach by Starting with Their DRIVE. Now, as you deepen your mastery of Assessing Their Needs, recognize the unique struggles each DRIVE faces:

D—Director: Directors struggle with feeling trapped, restricted, or controlled. They fiercely guard their freedom and independence, and any solution must reinforce their autonomy.

R—Relator: Relators battle the fear of letting people down, feeling disconnected, or unappreciated. Solutions for them must enhance relationships, build connections, and demonstrate sincere care and community.

I—Intellectual: Intellectuals wrestle with inefficiency, disorganization, or superficial solutions. They crave precision, clarity, and depth. Any solution must be structured, evidence-based, and thoughtfully presented.

V—Validator: Validators grapple with self-doubt, feeling overlooked, or undervalued. Solutions must affirm their worth, celebrate their strengths, and reinforce their unique contributions.

E—Executive: Executives face struggles around losing control, missing goals, or experiencing insecurity about future outcomes.

Solutions must clearly demonstrate reliability, control, predictability, and results.

By deeply understanding these struggles, you elevate your ability to connect, influence, and inspire trust. Don't rush—slow down. Listen not just to hear, but to truly learn. Let them tell you exactly how to close them. Your goal isn't just to solve a problem; it's to make your solution feel undeniably personal, powerful, and perfectly tailored.

When you Listen to Learn instead of Assume and Assault, you don't just make sales—you create loyal clients who feel seen, valued, and understood. You become more than a salesperson. You become indispensable.

Have you ever dreamed of standing center-stage with your favorite rock band, feeling the bass drum thumping in your chest? Or maybe you'd rather strut down the red carpet at Fashion Week—never mind that you're a quiet banker who's never worn Prada. How about rubbing elbows with royalty at Formula 1 in Monaco, or landing a walk-on role in your favorite TV series? Perhaps your ultimate fantasy is a private dinner at the feet of Michelangelo's David, serenaded by Andrea Bocelli himself.

Sound impossible? Not for Steve Sims and his company, Bluefish. Every day, Bluefish makes the extraordinary happen for their elite clientele. Want a trip to the International Space Station? Done. A private golf round with a certain green jacket champion? Easy. They once even transformed a client into James Bond for a weekend—complete with high-speed chases, secret agents, and, naturally, an Aston Martin.

Bluefish specializes in making dreams reality for those who refuse to settle for ordinary, for those bold enough to demand the incredible. But the magic isn't just in the extravagant feats they accomplish—it's in their relentless drive to uncover what truly ignites their clients' passion. Sims trains his salespeople to push past the superficial by asking "Why" at least three times. In his book, *Bluefishing*, Sims explains: "The first 'why' is what they think they think, the second 'why' is what they think you want to hear, and the third 'why' is what they FEEL."

Here's a captivating excerpt from his book that perfectly illustrates the profound power of deeply assessing someone's real needs:

Several years ago, my team got a call from a new client in New York. My people are terrific at new business calls like this, but this time my assistant put him on hold, buzzed me and said, "Look, I've got this guy on the line. There's something off. Can you jump on the call and take a listen?"

I love being on the front lines as much as I can, so without hesitating I picked up the phone and said, "Hey, how are you? This is Steve Sims. How can I help you?"

The voice on the phone was one of the least enthusiastic I've ever heard. Which is weird in my line of business. People call us to help make their wildest dreams happen, so usually we get people who are pretty fired up about their request.

However, this guy says, in monotone, "I need to get two tickets to the Playboy Mansion."

I said, "That's fine. We can make that happen for you. Let me get a pen so I can take some notes." I didn't need a pen, I needed to stall for a second, so I could think of a way to find this man's real reason for calling.

So, I start chatting with him, "Have you been to the Playboy Mansion before?"

"No, no I haven't." And there's still no excitement in this young man's voice about going to The Capital of Hedonism. None at all.

"Do you get to Los Angeles much?" I asked, just chit-chatting.

"Yeah, sometimes."

"Where do you go? North? South? Just stay in the hub?"

"Well, I like Hollywood, but I usually go up to Santa Barbara," and I could sense the voice was picking up in tempo.

So, I said, "You like Santa Barbara?"

"Oh, yeah, I love Santa Barbara."

"Really? I've been there a couple times," I commented.

"It was okay, I guess. What do you like so much about it?"

"Oh, well, the wine is incredible . . ." he said, and I could hear that he was smiling.

"Well, if you like wine, why aren't you heading up to Napa?" I asked.

That got him. "Oh, my God, I want to go to Napa so bad!" he said, almost like a little kid. And there it is. There's the excitement. There's the life on the line. Whew, I thought to myself, relieved. This, I can work with.

"Okay," I say, "we can send you to the Playboy Mansion, but first I really want to know why you haven't been to Napa?"

"Oh, I don't know! I always wanted to go to Napa." The guy was busting at the seams.

I thought to myself, I've got to get this guy to Napa. But I had to go through the original request protocol, so I went back to the Playboy project.

I ran through the planning for him. "We'll get you and a friend to the Playboy Mansion, you're at the Playboy Mansion for one night, let's look at your calendar."

He switched back to half-hearted right away.

When we were done scheduling, I said, "All right, back to Napa." And he perked up again. It was like flicking a switch on and off. The second I mentioned Playboy, we were in trouble. Mention Napa, the guy was up on cloud nine. Then it hit me. The real him came out when he was talking about Santa Barbara and Napa wine, but not about Playboy.

So, I asked, still chit-chatting, "What do you do for work?"

He said, "I'm a broker here in New York. I do this, I do that."

I said, "Got it. Now, I'm gonna go out on a limb here. And I mean no offense, and I have only acceptance, but, are girls not

really your thing? And damn, mate, why the hell do you want to go to Playboy?"

He fell quiet for a moment and I thought he was going to hang up on me. I was challenging him to be authentic with me, and that's not an easy thing for people to do.

He said finally, "I get so much peer pressure. I have to do something that is pure 100 percent testosterone."

I understood. I was rolling now. He was being sincere, and so now I could sincerely help. "So, the Playboy Mansion thing is not for you," I said. "You're doing it for everyone else in your office. Just to make them think you're straight. Is that it?"

"Yeah," he said softly.

"So, you're gonna fly over to LA and spend about fifteen to twenty thousand dollars, just to hopefully placate a few jerks in your office?" I asked, incredulous.

"Apparently." He sounded defeated. I couldn't take it.

So, I said, "I've got an idea for you. We're going to send you to Napa. Because that's where your heart is. I've already got a few people going to the Playboy Mansion, so I'll get you a couple of ticket stubs. You'll fly back from Napa with the ticket stubs, lay them on your desk, and no one's the wiser."

He was over the moon. We made that happen for him, and he became a client for many, many more years to come. Not because we sent him to Napa that one time, but because we listened to him and asked why."

Sims continues with,

If you can challenge your communication with someone, you in essence challenge the relationship that you'll experience as well. If you can get into that person's head and get beyond the shield, beyond the business card, beyond the pomp and ceremony, beyond the ego, beyond the fear of embarrassment, then you can deliver for them like never before. There's a person that wakes up, lives and breathes, feeds, goes to the toilet, loves their kids, and this essence is what they want. Once you can see that person, once you've got them, they don't go anywhere else. It's not because they like your flashy website, it's because you're communicating at a level they don't find anywhere else.

The heart of Sims' message is undeniable: If you truly want to dominate your sales game, stop accepting surface-level answers. Dive deeper. Challenge assumptions, disrupt their thinking, and dare to uncover their hidden truths. Because once you reach beyond the ego, the status, the fear—once you touch their core passion—you don't just win a client, you transform the relationship entirely.

Think about this: if your prospects already understood their real problems, they could simply Google the solution, ask TikTok or Reels, leverage AI, or dive into YouTube. Your job as a master salesperson isn't to solve the obvious problems—it's to uncover the hidden ones. Your real value lies in identifying and illuminating the issues they didn't even realize existed. When you discover the unknown, you become indispensable. This is the time where you master the art of deep, transformative insight.

The key isn't in fancy presentations or slick sales scripts; it's in your courage and curiosity to genuinely understand the human behind the request. This is how you create a connection no competitor can ever replicate.

Introducing the S.U.P.E.R. Method

Everything in this book represents a powerful collaboration between two passionate sales experts—but the S.U.P.E.R. Method is uniquely Bob Snyder's creation.

Long before we met, Bob developed, tested, and refined this transformative approach over more than forty years of coaching and mentoring 109,000+ sales professionals. Bob and his teams have generated hundreds of millions of dollars by mastering the art of assessing needs and leveraging solutions.

The S.U.P.E.R. Method encapsulates Bob's decades of proven success, giving you a precise framework to consistently achieve extraordinary results in your own sales career.

Every question in the S.U.P.E.R. Method is designed to uncover your prospect's emotional center—their Primary DRIVE. This is the heartbeat of every buying decision. It's what makes them care, what makes them act, and what gives your solution personal meaning.

As John C. Maxwell said, "Good questions inform. Great questions transform."

The S.U.P.E.R. Method helps you transform conversations into connection, problems into possibility, and resistance into results.

- **S—Situation:** Understand their current circumstances clearly and fully.

- **U—Understanding:** Dive into their mindset and perceptions about the situation.

- **P—Pain:** Identify the immediate challenges, frustrations, or discomfort they face.

- **E—Enlarge the Pain:** Amplify their awareness by exploring the consequences of not addressing their pain.

- **R—Release the Pain:** Provide tailored solutions that directly resolve the identified problems.

The S.U.P.E.R. Method isn't just a technique—it's your secret weapon for Assessing Their Needs. It gives you the ability to consistently engage at a deeper level, dramatically increase your value, and build relationships that last. Let's break down exactly how to apply it, step by powerful step.

Mastering S.U.P.E.R. Step by Step

As we unpack each step of the S.U.P.E.R. Method, think about a recent sales conversation you've had—or one you have coming up. Put yourself in that moment. Consider how each question naturally unfolds in your conversation.

The following questions aren't scripts—they're launchpads designed to ignite authentic conversations. They're designed to spark your own conversational style, encourage authenticity, and help you build genuine connections with your prospects. Customize them freely. Trust your instincts, stay true to your voice, and let each interaction become a genuine conversation—not just a sales pitch.

When you personalize your approach, you'll quickly notice how your prospects open up, appreciate your genuine interest, and ultimately move closer to saying yes.

S—Situation Questions

Get clear on what's happening in your prospect's world right now. Quickly understand their circumstances, where they're at, and what's led them to this moment.

Universal Questions:

- "Catch me up—what's going on with your situation right now?"
- "How long have you been dealing with this?"
- "Has anything changed recently that's made this more urgent or pressing for you?"

DRIVE-specific examples:

- Director: "What's feeling most restrictive or frustrating to you right now?"
- Relator: "How's this affecting the people around you—your family, your team?"

- **Intellectual:** "Walk me through your current approach—what parts aren't clicking for you?"
- **Validator:** "Do you feel you're being properly recognized in this situation, or is something missing?"
- **Executive:** "Tell me honestly, are you hitting your targets or is something getting in your way?"

U—Understanding Questions

Explore their perspective deeply. Go beyond surface-level answers to fully grasp their thoughts, motivations, and the real meaning behind their situation.

Universal Questions:

- "Why does fixing this feel important to you personally?"
- "How do you see this playing out if things stay the same?"
- "What do you feel is really at stake here—what makes this matter to you?"

DRIVE-specific examples:

- **Director:** "How is this holding you back from what you really want to experience?"
- **Relator:** "If we resolved this, what difference would it make to your team or family?"
- **Intellectual:** "What clarity do you feel you're still missing?"
- **Validator:** "What would resolving this mean for you personally—how would it change how you feel about yourself or your role?"
- **Executive:** "Bottom line, how is this impacting your ability to get the results you're after?"

P—Pain Questions

Uncover what's truly causing stress, frustration, or struggle. Pinpoint exactly what's holding them back or creating tension so you can address it directly.

Universal Questions:

- "What part of this feels like your biggest headache right now?"
- "Where are you feeling stuck or hitting a wall?"
- "What's keeping you up at night about this situation?"

DRIVE-specific examples:

- Director: "What's the one thing frustrating your ability to do things your way?"
- Relator: "Is there tension or frustration this is causing with your relationships or your team?"
- Intellectual: "Where's the confusion or uncertainty currently coming from?"
- Validator: "What about this situation is making you feel overlooked or undervalued?"
- Executive: "What's getting in the way of achieving what matters most to you?"

E—Enlarge the Pain Questions

Help your prospect vividly recognize the cost of staying stuck. Illuminate what's at stake if nothing changes, amplifying their motivation to act.

Universal Questions:

- "If nothing changes, where do you see this going?"
- "What's the cost if you keep doing things the same way?"
- "If we look six months down the road, what happens if this issue remains unresolved?"

DRIVE-specific examples:

- Director: "If this stays unresolved, how will it limit your freedom and control over your future?"
- Relator: "What will happen to your relationships if this issue continues to be ignored?"
- Intellectual: "How might today's small frustrations compound into bigger problems down the road?"
- Validator: "If things stay exactly as they are, how will that impact your confidence or sense of value?"
- Executive: "What future wins could slip through your fingers if we don't fix this now?"

R—Release the Pain Questions

Offer a clear, personalized solution that directly solves their problem. Show exactly how working with you removes their pain, creates relief, and moves them toward their ideal outcome.

Universal Questions:

- "Let's wave a magic wand for a second—what would a perfect solution look like to you?"
- "What's one thing we could do immediately to improve your situation?"
- "If we solved this today, how would things look different for you moving forward?"

DRIVE-specific examples:

- Director: "What would the ideal solution look like to fully empower you and remove these roadblocks?"
- Relator: "If we could address this perfectly, how would that transform your relationships or your team dynamic?"

- **Intellectual:** "What specific solution would finally give you the clarity and confidence you're after?"
- **Validator:** "Imagine feeling completely validated and recognized—what would need to change to get you there?"
- **Executive:** "How can we ensure this solution delivers exactly the outcomes you need to see?"

With the S.U.P.E.R. Method, you don't just sell—you connect deeply, solve meaningfully, and dominate your sales success.

You Get 100% of What You Don't Ask For

What's the true value of a question?

In *The One Thing*, Gary Keller said it brilliantly:

"Answers come from questions, and the quality of any answer is directly determined by the quality of the question. Ask the wrong question, get the wrong answer. Ask the right question, get the right answer. Ask the most powerful question possible, and the answer can be life-altering."

But can one simple question really change the world?

It was 1965 in Florida, and the scorching sun pressed relentlessly onto the University football field, sapping the players' strength with every passing minute. Sweat poured from their bodies like rivers. Despite drinking water, athletes were losing up to fourteen pounds during games without needing to urinate afterward. Something wasn't adding up—and nobody knew why.

Then, one sweltering afternoon, assistant football coach Dwayne Douglas asked kidney specialist Dr. Robert Cade a simple yet transformative question:

"Why are my players losing so much weight but not urinating after games?"

That one question seemed straightforward, maybe even trivial— but it was a riddle that would puzzle medical experts and ultimately revolutionize sports forever. Cade and his team plunged into months of intense research, uncovering a previously unseen truth: these players weren't just thirsty—they were dangerously dehydrated. Plain water simply wasn't enough. They were losing vital electrolytes and carbohydrates critical to their performance and recovery.

Fast forward to the 1967 Orange Bowl a couple of years later—Florida Gators versus Georgia Tech. It was the Gators' first-ever appearance, and expectations were sky-high. Yet, right out of the gate, disaster struck. Georgia Tech dominated the first half, running circles around Florida. The Gators dragged themselves off the field at halftime, exhausted, demoralized, and seemingly finished.

But in the locker room waited something new—something revolutionary. The players drank the newly developed concoction designed to rapidly replenish electrolytes and energy. Coach Ray Graves watched with hopeful skepticism, praying this strange, salty-sweet drink could somehow turn the tide.

And then, the impossible happened.

When the Gators stormed back onto the field, they were unrecognizable. While Georgia Tech began to slow and wilt under exhaustion, Florida surged forward, electrifying the crowd with unstoppable energy. The pivotal moment? A record-breaking ninety-four-yard touchdown run that left jaws dropping.

When the final whistle blew, Florida had done the unthinkable—they won their first Orange Bowl. Afterward, a bewildered Georgia Tech coach Bobby Dodd shook Graves' hand and confessed:

"We didn't have your drink. That made all the difference."

One question—one simple yet powerful question—changed sports forever. Cade and his team named their groundbreaking beverage after the Florida Gators' mascot. They called it Gatorade.

In 1983, the doctors behind Gatorade sold their creation to Quaker Oats for a staggering $220 million. In 2001, Pepsi acquired Quaker and Gatorade for a jaw-dropping $13 billion. Today, Gatorade generates over $7.2 billion in annual sales and proudly fuels seventy Division-1 colleges along with the NFL, NBA, MLB, and PGA.

All of this was born from a single question asked under the relentless Florida sun.

Never underestimate the transformative power of your questions. Each one holds untold potential. Your clients don't just buy products or services—they buy solutions to problems, clarity for confusion, relief from pain. But you can't provide any of that until you know exactly what drives them.

If you never ask, you'll never know.

And, as Einstein once revealed in his timeless wisdom: "If I had an hour to solve a problem and my life depended on it, I would use the first fifty-five minutes determining the proper questions to ask."

Every sales conversation is your Orange Bowl.

When you ask with intention and listen with precision, your prospects hand you the blueprint to close the deal. But insight alone isn't enough. Now it's time to take what they told you and reflect it back with clarity, confidence, and conviction. That's where the next step comes in—**Leverage Your Solutions.** Because once they've told you what matters most, your job is simple: show them exactly how your offer delivers it.

9

L—Leverage Your Solutions

I'm never giving my entire fleet of private jets to two twenty-nine-year-old kids with this cockamamie idea!" Rich Santulli, legendary founder and CEO of NetJets, wasn't merely rejecting Jesse Itzler and Kenny Dichter—he was kicking them out the door with force.

Just twelve minutes into their pitch, Santulli had heard enough. Security was called. Their PowerPoint, unfinished. Meeting over.

Itzler and Dichter had presented a revolutionary idea: a twenty-five-hour prepaid private jet card. Unlike NetJets' costly fractional ownership, their approach offered the luxury of private aviation without long-term commitments. There was just one major problem: these young men didn't own a single airplane.

Humiliated and disheartened, the pair exited the building questioning everything. But right before they left, Jim Jacobs, NetJets' president—the very person who had secured their meeting—pulled them aside:

"That was unbelievable," Jacobs told them. "Santulli doesn't give anybody twelve minutes. There's something powerful here. Bring this idea to life and come back next week."

Those words reignited their fire. Realizing a mere PowerPoint presentation wouldn't cut it, they knew they had to dramatically leverage their solutions.

Leveraging your solutions isn't just about presenting better ideas; it's about fundamentally shifting your prospect's existing associations to align directly with their DRIVE.

One week later, Itzler and Dichter returned—not with slides, but with undeniable proof. They transformed the boardroom into a live focus group, filled with exactly the high-net-worth individuals NetJets craved. NFL legend Carl Banks, Joseph "Run" Simmons of Run-D.M.C., a Wall Street heavyweight, and a renowned real estate mogul stepped forward, each declaring:

"We'd never buy a fraction of a jet—but we'd buy a twenty-five-hour jet card."

This wasn't just a pitch anymore; it was real customers demanding a better way. Santulli, immovable a week earlier, leaned in, reframing the entire concept in real-time. He no longer saw two inexperienced kids gambling with his fleet—he saw a wave of potential customers, an entirely new market now made impossible to ignore.

By the meeting's end, Santulli relented with a challenge: "If you're willing to put your own money on the line, let's see what happens."

Itzler and Dichter bet big, bought flight hours, and launched Marquis Jet. Within a year, their jet card program had more customers than NetJets itself. Between 2001 and 2010, Marquis Jet generated nearly $5 billion in sales, becoming the largest private jet card company globally, until NetJets acquired them outright.

Sales Are Built on Associations

At its core, every decision—whether it's choosing a brand, hiring someone, or making a purchase—comes down to our associations. People don't buy products or services; they buy what those things represent emotionally, based on their DRIVE.

- No one buys smartphones. They buy connection, productivity, and identity.
- No one buys streaming services. They buy control, entertainment, and escape.
- No one buys exercise gear. They buy transformation, community, and strength.

- No one buys clothes. They buy confidence, style, and belonging.
- No one buys computers. They buy efficiency, creativity, and possibilities.

Great salespeople don't compete on features—they dominate through associations.

Every buyer walks into a sale with pre-existing associations shaping their decisions. Some associations align perfectly with your offer, while others create objections, skepticism, or hesitation.

That's where creating a Reassociation is a game changer.

If prospects aren't buying, it's not because they don't need what you offer—it's because their current associations, shaped by their DRIVE, don't support the purchase. Most sales are lost not due to price or product, but because the offer isn't emotionally aligned with what the buyer truly wants. Your job isn't to push harder, memorize objection scripts, or flood them with information—it's to reframe how they see your offer. Because we buy emotionally, and justify logically.

The Law of Value

People will always exchange what they have for something they value more.

That's not just a sales truth—it's human nature. Every decision is a value equation. The moment your offer feels more valuable than their status quo, the sale tips in your favor. If they're hesitating, it's not about the price—it's about perception. You're not competing against dollars; you're competing against doubt, distraction, and disbelief. Shift the value, and you shift the decision. Your job isn't to lower the cost. Your job is to elevate the perceived value until *not buying* feels like the real risk.

This is why people spend $80,000 on a car they can't technically afford. Why they rack up credit card debt on brand-name gear. Why they upgrade the hotel room, go first-class, or add on that one extra feature. Because what they're getting feels worth more than what they're giving up.

Let's bring this to life with one of the boldest examples in modern branding:

Case Study:
Under Armour—From Fabric to Firepower

When Under Armour first launched, nobody was asking for moisture-wicking shirts. Nike and Adidas already owned the shelves. But Under Armour founder Kevin Plank (D/E) didn't sell clothing—he sold *performance*. He made compression gear a symbol of grit, toughness, and an athlete's edge. And he didn't try to be cheaper. He made Under Armour so valuable to the *identity* of a serious competitor that athletes couldn't afford to *not* wear it.

He didn't sell a shirt. He sold what the shirt *meant*—resilience, intensity, winning.

That's value. That's leverage. That's domination.

5 Brands That Master the Law of Value

1. **Apple**—They don't sell electronics. They sell status, simplicity, and creativity in your pocket.

2. **Lululemon**—They don't sell leggings. They sell the identity of someone who trains harder and lives better.

3. **Red Bull**—They don't sell energy drinks. They sell adrenaline, edge, and the power to push limits.

4. **Dyson**—They don't sell vacuums. They sell cutting-edge design, planet-friendly energy efficiency, and the pride of owning the best.

5. **LEGO**—They don't sell toys. They sell creativity, focus, and the joy of building something that lasts.

Each one could have competed on specs, pricing, or product features. They didn't. They rewired perception. They made their product *mean* something more.

If you want to leverage your solution, obey the Law of Value. Make your offer feel so aligned with your buyer's DRIVE, so emotionally irresistible, so psychologically loaded with positive gain, that saying no feels like an unjustifiable loss.

That's exactly what happened with Rich Santulli. His DRIVE was Executive/Intellectual (E/I)—motivated by proof, control, and systems. His initial association was blunt:

"Two kids with no aviation experience? No way."

Jesse Itzler (D/E) and Kenny Dichter (R/E) didn't argue or defend themselves. Instead, they transformed Santulli's emotional perception by showing real value. By placing influential, high-networth customers in front of him, they shifted his associations. Once Santulli saw real demand for their jet card model, he couldn't afford to ignore it.

The Law of Value tells us why people buy—but creating an emotional reassociation is how you make that value *feel* real. And no story shows that better than what happened with toothpaste.

In the early 1900s, most Americans didn't brush their teeth. It wasn't just a bad habit—it was a crisis. When the U.S. Army began drafting soldiers for World War I, thousands were rejected for one surprising reason: rotting teeth. Poor dental hygiene had become a national security threat.

It wasn't that people didn't know toothpaste existed. Advertisers had tried to sell it before. But there was no emotional connection. No urgency. No reason to care.

At the time, only 7% of Americans had toothpaste in their homes. It was just another forgotten product on the shelf—competing for attention and losing every time.

Then came Claude Hopkins.

One of the most influential advertisers of his era, Hopkins was an Intellectual/Validator (I/V), driven by mastery, structure, and the desire to make his work undeniably effective. He didn't just sell products, he sold identity. He tied habits to emotion, reward, and meaning. When he took on Pepsodent, he wasn't just facing a marketing challenge, he was up against a cultural wall. Telling people to brush to prevent cavities wasn't working. Logic wasn't enough.

So Hopkins looked deeper. He cracked open dental textbooks and discovered a phrase no one had ever thought to use in marketing: "mucin plaque"—a thin, invisible film that forms on your teeth every day. It didn't sound sexy, but it felt tangible. Because when you ran your tongue across your teeth, you could *feel it.*

That film became the hidden enemy. Not just a health risk—but the thing making your smile look dull.

Hopkins wrote ads that said:

"Just run your tongue across your teeth. Feel that film? That's what's making your smile look dingy."

It was simple. Immediate. Personal. And most importantly—emotional.

Brushing wasn't about avoiding cavities anymore. It was about revealing beauty.

Hopkins had reassociated the act of brushing your teeth with the identity of a confident, attractive person. And that changed everything.

Within five years, Pepsodent became a national phenomenon. A decade later, over 65% of households were brushing daily. Today, that number is over 90%—and many public health experts still credit Claude Hopkins for making brushing a national norm.

Here's the truth about what made it work:

He didn't win with logic.

He didn't win with features.

He won by reassociating a forgotten product with a powerful emotional reward.

If you take nothing else from this chapter, take this:

**"The Sale Will Not Happen
Until the Reassociation Occurs."**

Highlight that phrase. Tattoo it on every salesperson's forearm. Hang it in neon lights on your office walls. Scream it from the rooftops—and whatever you do, hide it from your competitors.

Why Every Sale Depends on a Reassociation

The only way to create real behavior change—the kind that sticks and sparks action—is through **Reassociation**: strategically leveraging your solution through the lens of their DRIVE. This isn't persuasion—it's precision. Reassociation rewires how they see the problem, the solution, and *you*. Look at any successful product, brand, or salesperson, and you'll see Reassociation at work.

- Yeti doesn't sell coolers. Those are a dime a dozen. They sell rugged adventure and durability.
- Warby Parker doesn't sell glasses. They sell style, affordability, and social impact.
- Chipotle doesn't sell burritos. They sell fresh, high-quality, ethically sourced food.

If your product isn't selling, it's usually not a product problem—it's a perception problem. The buyer already has an association that meets their DRIVE—but your offer hasn't created a stronger one.

The solution? A Reassociation.

Case Study:
Stanley—The Reassociation Revolution

For over 100 years, Stanley was a solid but unspectacular brand. Known for rugged, industrial thermoses built for construction workers and campers, it was the kind of product your grandfather swore by—reliable, tough, but nowhere near cool. In 2019, Stanley's annual sales hovered around $70 million. Respectable. But forgettable.

That all changed when Terence Reilly stepped in as President of Stanley in 2020.

Reilly, a bold Director/Executive(D/E), had already helped pull off a miracle at Crocs, turning a once-mocked brand into a cultural icon. He doesn't chase trends. He creates movements. Directors crave freedom—the freedom to reinvent, to challenge the status quo, to make people feel something entirely new. Executives, on the other hand, build strategies that win—reliable, repeatable playbooks designed to dominate. Reilly had both and he was about to unleash that DRIVE on Stanley.

The product that would change everything had been sitting on Stanley's shelves for years: the Quencher, a stainless steel tumbler first released in 2016. It flopped, ignored by retailers and overlooked by consumers. But Reilly didn't see a failure. He saw unrealized identity.

So he did what Directors do best: he tore up the old narrative.

Stanley didn't need to make a better cup. It needed to tell a better story . . . a more relevant one. Reilly repositioned the Quencher not as gear for the great outdoors but as an essential accessory for modern life. He leaned into sleek design, bold colorways, and a powerful emotional shift. The Quencher was no longer about durability. It was about belonging. Self-expression. Status.

He formed strategic partnerships with influencers on TikTok and Instagram. He

collaborated with style-focused blogs like *The Buy Guide*. He created drops, limited editions, and scarcity on purpose. This wasn't just marketing—it was Reassociation with a blueprint.

And it exploded.

By 2023, Stanley's sales skyrocketed from $70 million to $750 million. The Quencher became a viral juggernaut. The hashtag #StanleyCup racked up nearly 7 billion views on TikTok. Women across the country weren't just drinking from it—they were showing it off, coordinating it with outfits, and giving it as gifts. Stanley was no longer selling hydration—they were selling identity, lifestyle, and tribe.

Let's be clear: this wasn't accidental. This was a masterclass in Leveraging the Solution.

Reilly didn't try to out-feature competitors. He redefined the emotional meaning behind the product. He didn't sell a bottle. He sold a new association that aligned with the buyer's DRIVE.

Remember, people don't buy products—they buy what those products mean to them. And what they care about is shaped entirely by their Primary DRIVE. If you want to stand out in a crowded marketplace, you can't just stack features and bullet points. You need to Leverage Your Solutions by reshaping how your customer *feels* about what you offer.

Because when you make them feel something real, the sale takes care of itself.

Every DRIVE buys for a different emotional reason:

- **Directors** buy freedom, boldness, and challenge.
- **Relators** buy connection, meaning, and impact.
- **Intellectuals** buy depth, clarity, and knowledge.
- **Validators** buy confidence, recognition, and identity.
- **Executives** buy performance, control, and results.

A Reassociation is the act of taking your offer and aligning it with those specific emotions.

Here's a simple exercise to help you map it out:

1. Start by asking: *What is my product or service currently associated with?*

2. Then ask: *What does it need to be Reassociated with in order to speak to each DRIVE emotionally?*

Let's walk through an example using something simple: home security systems.

Most people's current association would be: Cameras. Alarms. Protection. Motion sensors.

They see a *tech product*—logical, functional, and a bit cold.

Reassociation by DRIVE:

- To a Director: *"Take back control of your space—freedom without fear."*
- To a Relator: *"Protect the people who matter most."*
- To an Intellectual: *"Peace of mind comes from a proven system you can trust—no more guessing."*
- To a Validator: *"You deserve to feel safe—and to be the one who protects the people you love."*
- To an Executive: *"An iron fortress guarding what you've built—even when you're not there."*

Now let's try it with something different: real estate education.

The likely current association would be: Education, strategies, and progress tracking.

Reassociation by DRIVE:

- To a Director: *"Learn how to fire your boss, work from anywhere, and design your own path through investing."*
- To a Relator: *"Build generational wealth, invest in your family's future, and create impact in your community."*

- To an **Intellectual:** *"Access to deep training, formulas, tools, and strategies that make you a smarter, more efficient investor."*

- To a **Validator:** *"Earn status in the community, become a mentor, and gain confidence by mastering a respected skill."*

- To an **Executive:** *"Build an empire, run the numbers, take calculated risks, and become the CEO of your own portfolio."*

Once you see it, you'll never unsee it. Your product doesn't change, but the way it *connects* to the buyer does. That's the power of Reassociation.

Reassociation: Your Turn

Now it's time to take this tool into your own hands. Think about how your product or service is currently perceived. What is it *associated* with? What do people assume about it right now?

Then, ask yourself the most important question of all:

"How do I want my product to feel emotionally to each customer's DRIVE?"

To help you get started, here's a simple Reassociation Cheat Sheet. Use it as a guide to help you shape your message for each type of buyer.

Reassociation Cheat Sheet: Emotional Hooks by DRIVE

- Director:
  - *Freedom, control, bold action, adventure, breaking the mold*
  - Speak to their desire to lead, choose their own path, and avoid limits.

- Relator:
  - *Connection, trust, legacy, meaning, influence through service*
  - Speak to the relationships they care about and how your offer helps them serve, support, or strengthen others.

- **Intellectual:**
  - *Understanding, insight, mastery, structure, confidence in the method*
  - Speak to their need for clarity, logic, and the pursuit of better systems.

- **Validator:**
  - *Respect, recognition, personal confidence, belonging, inner strength*
  - Speak to who they want to become—and how your offer helps them feel seen, strong, and valuable.

- **Executive:**
  - *Results, performance, control, leadership, winning*
  - Speak to what they'll accomplish, what they'll build, and how your offer helps them run the show.

By now, you've done the hard work that most salespeople ignore. You **Started with their DRIVE**—so you know what emotionally motivates them. You **Assessed their Needs**—so you understand their pain points and priorities. And now, in **Leveraging Your Solutions**, your goal is to create a Reassociation that speaks directly to both: what they want most, and what they're struggling with.

But here's the question most salespeople never ask: *Is this solution emotionally aligned with their DRIVE?*

That's where the **Trial Close** comes in. Before you move forward, you need to check for alignment. This isn't done with pressure and it's certainly not a pitch. It's simply a question.

This is where most salespeople blow it. They go straight from presentation to close without ever stopping to ask, "Are we on the same page?" Then they're blindsided when objections show up out of nowhere. That's why every leveraged solution should end with a Trial Close. It's not about closing the deal just yet—it's about opening the door to clarity.

In order to accomplish this, you don't need to memorize robotic lines or force words that don't feel like you. These aren't magic phrases. They're simply starting points to help you check alignment in your own voice and rhythm. The key is to use language that feels natural to you and resonates with them.

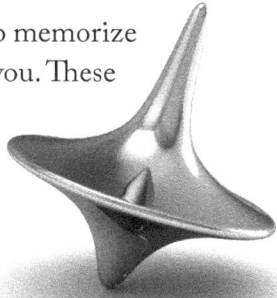

Remember: you sell to the Primary DRIVE, but you close to the Secondary. The Primary DRIVE gets them emotionally excited—it's what made them lean in. But it's the Secondary DRIVE that has to make sense of the decision. The Trial Close is your moment to check in with both. Does this solution still feel aligned emotionally (Primary)? And does it make sense logically (Secondary)? If either one is out of sync, hesitation will creep in. But when both are aligned, you're nearly there.

Here are seven Trial Close questions to keep in your back pocket:

1. *"Does this feel like the kind of solution you've been looking for?"*

2. *"If we could make this work within your budget/timeline, would you feel good about moving forward?"*

3. *"Is this headed in the right direction for you?"*

4. *"What part of this feels most aligned with what you need right now?"*

5. *"Does this sound like it would solve the challenge we talked about earlier?"*

6. *"If you had to make the call today, what would be holding you back?"*

7. *"Where do you feel hesitation?"*

You don't need to ask them all. One well-timed question is often enough to surface what's really going on—whether it's a green light, a hesitation, or a concern that needs attention. And when a concern does surface? That's your cue to move into the next step in the DRIVE S.A.L.E.S. System: **E—Eliminate Their Concern.**

10

E—Eliminate Their Concern

There was one billion dollars on the line. That wasn't a projection or guess. It was real money bleeding out of the system. Jon Stegner needed to do one thing: convince a room full of seasoned executives, factory foremen, and procurement managers to question the way they'd always done business.

He wasn't up against open resistance. Instead, he faced something harder: unspoken doubt. The kind of subtle pushback every salesperson knows too well. No one argued with him, yet behind the polite nods and quiet stares was a wall of deeply rooted habits and silent concerns. Spreadsheets weren't going to move these people. Power-Points weren't going to shake them, either. If Stegner wanted to break through, he needed something stronger than logic—he needed to create a moment they could feel.

Stegner saw the opportunity: if the company could cut its purchasing costs by just 2%, they'd save over a billion dollars in five years. But the data alone wasn't enough. They didn't *feel* the problem. So he decided to do something bold—he chose a single product everyone in the company used: gloves. He asked an intern to find out how many kinds of gloves were being ordered across the company's factories, and at what cost. The results were staggering. 424 different kinds of gloves. Each factory had its own suppliers, its own pricing, and no oversight. The same exact glove could cost $5 in one factory and $17 in another.

When he made this discovery, Stegner didn't send out a report. He chose to create an experience. He reserved the executive boardroom and piled all 424 gloves onto the center table. Each one was tagged with the price and factory it came from. Then he invited the division presidents to come take a look.

When they entered the room, they didn't say a word. They just stared. The table—normally reserved for order and structure—was buried in a chaotic mountain of gloves. Some executives began walking the perimeter, scanning the tags. That's when the reality started to land. One man held up two nearly identical gloves, one marked $3.22, the other $10.55. He turned to Stegner and asked, "We're really buying all these?"

Stegner simply nodded. "Yes. We are."

And in that moment, something shifted. There was no argument. No pushback. No defensiveness. What they saw didn't just make sense—it hit them. *Emotionally,* they felt the absurdity, the waste, and the lack of control. *Logically,* they saw the proof, the pattern, and the system failure. Stegner hadn't just presented a better process—he had created a moment that gave them emotional urgency and the logical clarity to act.

That glove display became a company legend. Stegner's display was a traveling roadshow that toured division after division. It didn't just inform—it transformed. It eliminated doubt by showing value. It eliminated resistance by creating alignment. And it proved something that's true in every sale: when you create the right kind of moment, objections don't need to be overcome. They disappear.

For decades, salespeople have been taught to treat objections like battles. They believe the only solution is to learn the scripts, memorize the rebuttals, and don't take no for an answer. You have to say the right thing, spin it the right way, and keep pushing until they cave.

But here's the problem—that approach doesn't work anymore. And if we're being honest, it probably never really felt right in the first place. Because every time you try to "handle" an objection with a pre-rehearsed line or a clever comeback, something happens: the energy shifts. The customer leans back. The connection cracks. You're still talking, but they're already gone.

That's because objections aren't resistance—they're requests for more conviction and clarity. Unfortunately, this is where the typical salesperson misses the message. When the client says, "It's too expensive," they're not rejecting your price—they're protecting their priorities. When they say, "Let me think about it," they're not stalling—they're telling you they haven't connected the dots yet. And when they say, "I don't think now's the right time," they're really saying, "I'm not convinced this is the right move for me."

What most people call objections are really just unmet needs in disguise. The concern is not truly the problem—the concern is the customer trying to tell you what they *still need* to believe, feel, or understand before they can move forward. The moment you see it that way, everything changes. You stop reacting and you start listening. Then, you can finally start speaking their language.

Let's talk about the big three objections: Time. Energy. Money. The holy trinity of hesitation. Every salesperson has heard them. Every customer has used them. And they sound so reasonable. So logical. So final. But here's the truth: they're not real barriers—they're the camouflage people use to avoid revealing what's really going on.

Think about it. Have you ever heard someone say they "don't have time" . . . only to watch them spend an entire weekend bingeing a television show, scrolling Instagram, or standing in line for overpriced coffee? Or someone might claim that they "don't have the energy," yet somehow they're up at 5 a.m. hitting the gym, coaching their kid's team, or planning a vacation? And money? Please. People "can't afford it" until the right truck, trip, or tech gadget shows up—and then suddenly, the funds magically appear.

When people want something badly enough, they make time, they find energy, and they get resourceful with their money. Those aren't unbreakable objections—they're just placeholders for something deeper: a *lack of perceived value.* A lack of alignment. A lack of emotional certainty or logical clarity.

Objections like "I don't have time" or "It's too expensive" aren't the problem. They're symptoms. And if all you do is respond to the symptom, you miss the cause. You get stuck in back-and-forth battles, trying to justify price or argue for urgency, when the truth is the customer's not convinced it's worth it *for them.* Not yet.

Remember this: Time, energy, and money are not the issues. Value is.

If the customer doesn't see how this helps them win, feel secure, grow, connect, or stand out, they'll protect what they have instead. That protection usually shows up as a polite, "I need to think about it."

When you understand this concept, objections will stop feeling like roadblocks. They become invitations to add more value—not more pressure.

So if time, energy, and money aren't the real problem . . . what is?

By now we've discussed this phrase in detail: *We buy emotionally and justify logically.* This is a law of human behavior. And if you understand it, you hold the key to eliminating objections forever.

This is where you hone in on the power of DRIVE that we've already built the foundation for: your client has a Primary DRIVE, which is emotional, and a Secondary DRIVE, which is logical. The Primary DRIVE is their emotional GPS. And depending on who you're talking to, that emotion isn't random—it's one of five deep desires: either freedom, connection, understanding, recognition, or control. But

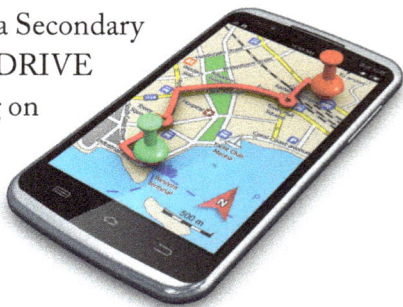

the Secondary DRIVE? That's just as important. It's their internal logic filter. It's how they justify the decision to themselves and others.

When a customer hesitates, it's not about price or timing. It's about a gap. Sometimes that gap is emotional—they don't feel confident, aligned, or excited. That's a Conviction Gap. Other times it's logical—they don't yet see how it fits into their world. That's a Clarity Gap. And until both gaps are closed, they won't move.

You're not just selling a product—you're guiding a decision. And every decision is powered by two forces:

Conviction + Clarity = Action.

It's not one or the other. It's both.

Conviction is emotional. It's that gut feeling that says: *This is what I've been looking for.*

Clarity is logical. It's that mental click that tells you: *I see exactly how this fits into my world and why it makes sense right now.*

Want the truth behind every real buying decision?

Emotion drives the decision. Logic gives it permission.

Look at Stegner. He didn't try to win those people over with spreadsheets or charts. He gave them an experience they could feel. The gloves piled on the table created an immediate emotional reaction that declared: *"We're bleeding money."* That was conviction. But he didn't stop there. The tags, the pricing, and the comparisons created clarity. They didn't just feel the problem—they could see the solution in front of them.

That's the advantage of Stegner's DRIVE—Executive/Intellectual (E/I). He wasn't just a numbers guy. He knew the system had to make sense *and* feel undeniable. He didn't push. He didn't pitch. He gave them conviction they couldn't ignore and clarity they couldn't unsee.

That's how you eliminate concern, by closing the gap that's holding them back. Because when a customer *feels* the conviction and *sees* the clarity? Action becomes automatic.

So the next time someone objects, don't ask yourself, *How do I overcome this?* Instead, consider, *Which gap am I closing right now— their conviction or their clarity?*

And when you bring both, you actually don't have to close them. They'll close themselves.

Closing the Conviction Gap

This is the emotional side of the sale, when the customer *feels it.* When something inside them says, *This is what I need.* When the heart leans forward before the head can even catch up.

But when conviction is missing, it shows up as hesitation. Not because the product is wrong but because the *feeling* isn't right. The customer doesn't feel seen, understood, or connected to the outcome. So they protect themselves with polite resistance.

It sounds like:

- *"I need to think about it."*
- *"This just isn't the right time."*
- *"Let me sit with it for a bit."*

And here's what makes the Conviction Gap tricky: they might not even know why they're hesitating. That's what makes this issue emotional. It lives below the surface.

This is where knowing your client's Primary DRIVE becomes your advantage. After all, people don't buy because you believe in the product—they buy when it hits something real inside of them. When it speaks to who they are and what they're chasing. That's not persuasion. That's connection.

- A Director doesn't feel it until they believe it will lead to more freedom, more creativity, or a life that feels fully lived.
- A Relator doesn't feel it until they sense trust, connection, and a chance to serve or belong.

- An **Intellectual** doesn't feel it until it aligns with their standards or helps them experience deeper understanding.
- A **Validator** doesn't feel it until they feel respected, appreciated, or personally recognized.
- An **Executive** doesn't feel it until it clearly helps them win, solve, or protect something they care about.

The Conviction Gap is closed by helping the customer see themselves in the solution. It's not about what it does—it's about what it *means*.

- If a **Director** doesn't feel the freedom, they won't engage.
- If a **Relator** doesn't feel the connection, they'll keep their distance.
- If an **Intellectual** doesn't feel the clarity, they won't move.
- If a **Validator** doesn't feel seen, they won't say yes.
- If an **Executive** doesn't feel the win, they'll walk away.

Your job is simple, but powerful: build conviction.

- Paint the emotional payoff.
- Speak their DRIVE language.
- Reassure the *person*, not just the buyer.
- Most of all, help them *feel* what their future looks like on the other side of saying yes.

When conviction is present, objections start falling away. They stop needing convincing because now, they believe.

The Clarity Gap

While conviction is all about what your customer *feels*, clarity is about what they *understand*. It's the logical part of the decision that has to make sense on paper *and* in their world.

When clarity is missing, it's not because the customer doesn't believe in you—it's because they can't quite see how it fits. Something's fuzzy. Unanswered. They don't know what happens next, or how this connects to their goals, their resources, or their reality.

It sounds like:

- *"I just need to think through the details."*
- *"Let me run the numbers."*
- *"Can you send me something to look over?"*

These aren't stalls—they're signals of disconnection. They're saying, *"I want to believe . . . but I don't fully see it yet."*

That's the Clarity Gap.

And this is where the Secondary DRIVE becomes your guide.

- A Director (as a Secondary) needs to see how this gives them more freedom, fewer restrictions, and lets them move fast.
- A Relator (as a Secondary) wants to know how this will impact people they care about or serve.
- An Intellectual (as a Secondary) needs to understand the process, the structure, and the logic behind it.
- A Validator (as a Secondary) wants to be reassured that this decision makes them look wise or worthy in the eyes of others.
- An Executive (as a Secondary) needs to see the ROI—how it helps them win, protect, or solve a problem with clear next steps.

When someone has conviction but lacks clarity, they'll want to buy . . . but they won't let themselves. The emotion is there but the logic hasn't caught up.

So what do you do? You slow down and simplify. You help them connect the dots.

Ask:

- *"What part still feels unclear?"*

- *"What would make this easier to see in action?"*
- *"What would give you the confidence to move forward?"*

Then listen well. Don't fill the space with features. Fill it with clarity. Because when the logic clicks, the resistance fades.

The Objection Decoder: How to Tell What They're Really Saying

Objections don't show up with name tags. Your customer won't say, "Hi, I'm having a Conviction Gap today." Instead, they'll give you surface-level reasons that you can identify—logical on the outside, but emotionally loaded underneath. If you want to eliminate concerns before they stall the sale, you need to know what you're actually hearing. This cheat sheet gives you a quick-glance decoder to spot whether you're dealing with a Conviction Gap (emotional) or a Clarity Gap (logical) so you can speak to the real need hiding behind the resistance.

Objection Language: Conviction vs. Clarity

Conviction Gap (Emotional)	Clarity Gap (Logical)
"It just doesn't feel right."	"I don't fully understand how this works."
"I'm not sure this is me."	"What exactly do I get?"
"I don't feel excited about it."	"Can you walk me through the details again?"
"Something's off—I can't explain it."	"How long does the setup take?"
"This isn't clicking for me yet."	"What's the timeline look like?"
"It feels like a risk."	"I need to talk to someone on my team."
"I don't know if I trust this yet."	"What are the next steps after I say yes?"
"Let me think about it." *(emotional hesitation)*	"Can you send me something to review?"
"I'm not sure this lines up with what I'm about."	"Does this integrate with what we're already using?"
"I don't feel ready yet."	"How do we handle this if ___ happens?"

SHOW. Don't Tell:
The Fastest Way to Eliminate Doubt

Once you know whether the gap is emotional or logical, the next step is to close it—and nothing closes faster than SHOW. Don't Tell. But here's the twist: SHOW isn't just a principle. It's a playbook. It stands for *Social Proof, Hands On, Offer Samples,* and *Wow Factor*—four tactical moves designed to create conviction without saying a word. This is how you bypass resistance, eliminate doubt, and get straight to belief. When you SHOW, you don't argue—you prove. You don't pitch—you demonstrate. You let your customer feel the win for themselves. SHOW meets them where they are and moves them forward.

S—Social Proof: Let Others Do the Talking

People trust others more than they trust you. That's not personal—it's psychology. *Social Proof* is the emotional and logical reassurance that comes from seeing others already doing what you're asking your customer to do. It signals safety, credibility, and alignment—without you ever needing to say, "Trust me."

Want to see it done brilliantly? Walk into any 5 Guys restaurant, anywhere in the world. You won't find sleek billboards or celebrity endorsements. What you'll see are walls lined with magazine reviews, customer raves, and third-party praise—all shouting one message: *"You can trust this."*

They don't sell burgers with hype. They sell them with proof.

From London to Los Angeles, the decor never changes. Red and white tiles. A simple menu. And article after article bragging about their food. That's not coincidence—it's strategy. It's *Social Proof* doing the heavy lifting. You walk in, you see the evidence, and before your brain can analyze it, your gut says, *This place must be good.*

Social Proof eliminates doubt before it has a chance to speak. It's confidence, on display.

You don't have to say, "I'm the best." Just SHOW that others already believe it. When the customer sees people like them getting real results, an internal switch flips: *If it worked for them . . . maybe it'll work for me, too.*

H—Hands On: Let Them Feel It Themselves

There's a moment when curiosity turns into conviction—and it rarely happens through explanation alone. That moment is earned through experience. That's the power of *Hands On.*

Look at Pepsi in the 1970s. Coke had the market, the brand, and the swagger. Pepsi was the underdog, trailing in every category. Then came one of the boldest marketing moves of the decade: the Pepsi Challenge.

They didn't run ads claiming to taste better. They let people prove it to themselves. This was a historic, blind taste test—Pepsi vs. Coke. No labels. No cues. Just real people and real reactions. Pepsi kept winning.

Instead of talking about their flavor, they let the customer experience it.

And it changed everything. Pepsi didn't just steal attention—they stole belief. *Hands On* became their edge. Sales skyrocketed, and so did their brand momentum. In the years that followed, Pepsi acquired Pizza Hut, Taco Bell, KFC, Gatorade, and more—growing into a $60+ billion empire. Why? Because they stopped trying to *tell* people what to believe and let them taste it for themselves.

Whether you sell a product or a service, the principle is the same: the best pitch is the one they participate in.

Merely talking about your solution isn't enough. Give them a moment to feel it, touch it, test it, and try it.

- Let them walk through the process.
- Put the tool in their hands.

- Roleplay a real scenario.
- Give them a small win before the big yes.

Because when someone experiences the win firsthand, their belief doesn't need to be built—it's already there.

O—Offer Samples: Let Them Taste the Win

There's a reason Costco's sample tables are always crowded—samples *work*. They bypass skepticism and give people a taste of what's possible. In a world filled with noise, offering even a bite-sized experience builds belief faster than a dozen claims ever could.

Snack Factory knew this when they launched an unknown, oddly shaped product called *Pretzel Crisps*. It wasn't quite a chip, not quite a pretzel. The name alone left people scratching their heads. So instead of running ads, they hit the streets with one goal: *get people to taste it.*

They handed out free samples at grocery stores, events, and trade shows. The result? Between 25% to 30% of people who tried it bought it on the spot. The strategy turned an untested snack into a national brand, now sold in over 20,000 stores including Target and Walmart.

Why did it work? Because of one word: reciprocity. Behavioral economist Dan Ariely explains, "When someone gives you something—even a tiny chocolate—you feel a surprisingly strong urge to do something back." Samples don't just activate curiosity—they trigger a micro-commitment. You're no longer a spectator. You've tasted the win.

Here's the key: A sample doesn't have to be edible.

You can sample insight in a workshop. Sample results in a case study. Sample value in a free audit, a walkthrough, or a preview. Whether it's software, real estate, coaching, or curriculum, when people can experience the benefit, belief skyrockets.

So ask yourself:

- What can they try before they buy?
- What can you let them feel instead of just hear?
- What micro-win could tip the scale?

A sample turns doubt into action—because it lets the customer take a test drive into belief.

W—Wow Factor: Make the Moment Unforgettable

Some moments get attention. Others stop time. The Wow Factor is that second kind—the kind that makes people freeze, lean in, and say, "What was that?"

This step is not about being flashy—it's about being unforgettable. It's when your product or message is so unexpected, so visually gripping, or so emotionally undeniable that people can't look away. They don't need to be told. They've seen it for themselves—and now, they believe.

Tom Dickson, CEO of Blendtec, was doing something most execs wouldn't touch: jamming a 2×2 piece of wood into a blender just to see what would happen. George Wright, their VP of Marketing, watched it splinter and thought, This could work.

Dickson, a bold Director/Executive (D/E), wasn't afraid to break the rules. Wright, an Intellectual/Validator (I/V), saw the genius in the chaos. A blender eating an iPhone wasn't a stunt: it was a story. So, they spent $50 on a lab coat, a camera, and a bag of random objects: marbles, glow sticks, a Happy Meal—even an iPhone.

When they posted these extreme videos online, they went viral.

"Will It Blend?" became an internet juggernaut. The sight of an iPhone being pulverized in seconds didn't need explanation. It screamed durability, power, and fun. No pitch. No hard sell. Just pure, unfiltered *Wow Factor* in action. Sales jumped 500%. Site traffic exploded 650%. And suddenly, Blendtec wasn't just a blender—it was a phenomenon.

©Courtesy Photo

The lesson? Don't tell people what your product can do. Show them in a way they'll never forget.

Ask yourself:

- What would shock someone into *believing*?

- What's the most outrageous, visually striking, or emotionally resonant way to prove your point?

- If your product had a viral moment, what would it look like?

When done right, the *Wow Factor* doesn't just grab attention—it converts.

You've now walked through **S.A.L.E.** and at this point, you should realize: This is where the transformation happens.

- **You Started with Their DRIVE** to uncover what emotionally motivates them.

- **You Assessed Their Needs** to speak to their real problems—not your pitch.
- **You Leveraged Your Solutions** through powerful Reassociation, aligning it with what they care about most.
- **You Eliminated Their Concern** by closing the Conviction and Clarity gaps that keep buyers stuck.

But here's the part most people miss: the Trial Close isn't a one-time event. It's a rinse-and-repeat tool. Every time you introduce a new insight, offer a new angle, or add more value—you check alignment. You don't push forward blindly. You test for belief. You test for buy-in. And if concern shows up again? You close the gap—again.

Now comes the final move: **Sell Them Their DRIVE Solution.**

11

S—Sell Them Their DRIVE Solution

With a $250,000 contract on the line, the pressure was suffocating. At the time, DRIVE was still in its infancy, and I was fighting to get it off the ground while raising a young family. We were doing fine, but this client lived in a different stratosphere. And when you play at that level, "fine" doesn't cut it.

The client? A wildly successful CEO and serious exotic car collector. The kind of guy who didn't just drive Lamborghinis—he lived like one. Loud, bold, and built to win. He was a classic Director/Validator, obsessed with big vision, fast execution, and being seen as the sharpest guy in any room.

And now he was looking at me, waiting for a pitch. But I knew a generic contract or a polished proposal wouldn't land. Not with him. If I wanted to win him over, I couldn't just talk. I had to match his energy and validate his brilliance. I needed to SHOW him something that felt made for him. Something bold. Something undeniable.

I bought a 2′ × 3′ poster board and turned it into a full-on visual roadmap—his business as the car, the goals as the road ahead, and the finish line as a fleet of cutout Lamborghinis and Ferraris from the DuPont Registry. It looked like a kid's science fair project, but I had a feeling it would work. I had it laminated, cut into puzzle pieces, and overnighted to him in a dramatic, custom package.

By 11:57 a.m. the next day, he called me, fired up and ready to start. He didn't just say yes. He said, "This is exactly how I think!" It was one of the fastest closes I've ever had.

So, naturally, knowing this approach worked, I repeated it.

I created another custom version of the same concept, tailored to another CEO that my new client just introduced me to. This was another car guy. Another potential big win. And this one had an even bigger company. Same overnight delivery. Similar puzzle presentation.

But this time . . . silence.

A few days passed. Nothing. A week went by. Still nothing. Finally, I called his assistant. She hesitated, then explained, "He got it. When he opened the box and the puzzle pieces fell on his desk . . . he looked at them, said, 'I don't have time for this,' and slid it into his drawer."

My heart fell. The deal was dead. I didn't even get a conversation.

That second CEO was an Executive/ Intellectual. He wasn't wired for creativity—he was wired for efficiency. He wanted a clean strategy, backed by logic, structure, and a clear ROI. The puzzle didn't spark curiosity—it triggered impatience. What felt like a breakthrough to one client felt like a waste of time to another.

That's when it hit me: this wasn't about having a universal pitch. It was about having the *right* one. Their DRIVE is the difference.

My strategy landed a dream client in under twenty-four hours. The same strategy lost a quarter-million-dollar opportunity forever.

Same product. Same industry. Same love of cars. Totally different DRIVEs.

This is where DRIVE gives you the edge—it helps you stop pitching and start connecting.

Now that you understand how powerful this approach can be, selling to the Primary (emotional) and closing to the Secondary (logic), it's time to put it to work. What follows is your complete guide to the 20 Primary and Secondary DRIVE combinations. Think of it as your GPS—a framework for crafting a pitch that speaks to what they feel and how they think. These aren't scripts. They're starting points to help you sell with clarity, confidence, and connection.

D/R—Director/Relator

- **Primary DRIVE (Director):** Motivated by freedom, creativity, purpose, and overcoming challenges. They want to lead, break the mold, and live boldly.
- **Secondary DRIVE (Relator):** Evaluates decisions based on relationships and personal impact. They ask: *"How does this affect the people I care about?"*
- **Sell to the Emotion:** Speak to their desire to break free, do something bold, and chart a new path with meaning.
- **Close with Logic:** Highlight how the solution deepens relationships, supports others, and creates a meaningful legacy.

D/I—Director/Intellectual

- **Primary DRIVE (Director):** Motivated by freedom, creativity, purpose, and overcoming challenges.
- **Secondary DRIVE (Intellectual):** Uses knowledge, insight, and structure to evaluate decisions. They ask: *"Is this smart, proven, and clear?"*
- **Sell to the Emotion:** Speak to their desire to break free, challenge norms, and create something revolutionary.
- **Close with Logic:** Provide frameworks, data, or a proven method that confirms the decision is intelligent and strategic.

D/V—Director/Validator

- **Primary DRIVE (Director):** Motivated by boldness, living fully, and experiencing purpose-driven freedom.
- **Secondary DRIVE (Validator):** Judges decisions based on personal worth, recognition, and respect. They ask: *"Will this elevate me or validate my worth?"*
- **Sell to the Emotion:** Speak to their desire to rise above, lead boldly, and break barriers.
- **Close with Logic:** Show how the decision will earn recognition, boost visibility, or affirm their expertise.

D/E—Director/Executive

- **Primary DRIVE (Director):** Motivated by freedom, challenges, and bold self-expression.
- **Secondary DRIVE (Executive):** Focuses decisions on outcomes, control, and measurable success. They ask: *"Does this help me win?"*
- **Sell to the Emotion:** Speak to their desire to lead, disrupt, and take on meaningful challenges.
- **Close with Logic:** Outline a clear plan, measurable KPIs, and outcomes that demonstrate a path to victory.

R/D—Relator/Director

- **Primary DRIVE (Relator):** Motivated by connection, meaning, influence, and service. They want to feel close to people and make an authentic difference.
- **Secondary DRIVE (Director):** Evaluates decisions based on personal freedom, bold action, and alignment with their purpose.

They ask: *"Will this help me do something meaningful on my own terms?"*

- **Sell to the Emotion:** Speak to their desire to connect, uplift others, and create impact in relationships, teams, or communities.
- **Close with Logic:** Show how this allows them to lead in their own way, expand their influence, and have the freedom to serve people in their way.

R/I—Relator/Intellectual

- **Primary DRIVE (Relator):** Motivated by connection, meaning, and service.
- **Secondary DRIVE (Intellectual):** Uses clarity, structure, and understanding to evaluate decisions. They ask: *"Does this make sense, and does it align with what I value?"*
- **Sell to the Emotion:** Speak to their heart—share how the solution strengthens relationships, helps people they care about, or creates something meaningful.
- **Close with Logic:** Provide clarity, structure, and thoughtful explanation to show how this aligns with their mission or values.

R/V—Relator/Validator

- **Primary DRIVE (Relator):** Motivated by connection, belonging, and impact.
- **Secondary DRIVE (Validator):** Judges decisions based on identity, respect, and recognition. They ask: *"Will this reflect who I am and how I want to be seen?"*
- **Sell to the Emotion:** Tap into their desire to serve and support others. Show how this brings people together or helps someone they care about.

- **Close with Logic:** Reassure them that this decision affirms their identity, strengthens their value in others' eyes, or helps them feel appreciated.

R/E—Relator/Executive

- **Primary DRIVE (Relator):** Motivated by deep relationships, connection, and service.
- **Secondary DRIVE (Executive):** Evaluates decisions by their impact, efficiency, and measurable outcomes. They ask: *"Will this get results for the people I care about?"*
- **Sell to the Emotion:** Focus on how your offer creates positive outcomes for the people they serve—their team, family, and/or community.
- **Close with Logic:** Give a clear path to execution, timelines, and proof that this will actually help those they want to help.

I/D—Intellectual/Director

- **Primary DRIVE (Intellectual):** Motivated by understanding, knowledge, clarity, and growth. They want things to make sense.
- **Secondary DRIVE (Director):** Evaluates decisions based on personal freedom, boldness, and independent exploration. They ask: *"Can I explore this on my own terms?"*
- **Sell to the Emotion:** Tap into their curiosity. Show how your offer helps them go deeper and learn more, or master a concept, system, or skill.
- **Close with Logic:** Highlight how they can apply it independently, make it their own, and use it as a tool for personal or intellectual freedom.

I/R—Intellectual/Relator

- **Primary DRIVE (Intellectual):** Motivated by knowledge, insight, and systems. They want to understand how things work and why.
- **Secondary DRIVE (Relator):** Judges decisions by their impact on relationships, connection, and meaningful service. They ask: *"Will this help me make a meaningful difference?"*
- **Sell to the Emotion:** Show how your solution gives them clarity or insight that makes life simpler, healthier, or more effective.
- **Close with Logic:** Tie their learning to people—explain how this knowledge helps them teach, support, or improve lives around them.

I/V—Intellectual/Validator

- **Primary DRIVE (Intellectual):** Motivated by truth, clarity, and mastery.
- **Secondary DRIVE (Validator):** Evaluates decisions based on alignment with their identity, self-worth, and personal growth. They ask: *"Does this align with who I am and how I want to grow?"*
- **Sell to the Emotion:** Focus on how your offer makes sense, is well thought-out, and empowers them to be more skilled, more precise, or more capable.
- **Close with Logic:** Show how this decision reinforces their identity—how it positions them as smart, respected, and personally elevated.

I/E—Intellectual/Executive

- **Primary DRIVE (Intellectual):** Motivated by understanding, precision, and learning.

- **Secondary DRIVE (Executive):** Considers decisions based on practicality, productivity, and measurable outcomes. They ask: *"Does this work? Will its application help me win?"*
- **Sell to the Emotion:** Lead with insight—demonstrate how your solution brings clarity or structure to a problem they've been trying to solve.
- **Close with Logic:** Walk them through how it works, how to implement it, and the specific results it can deliver. Show the specific system that creates success.

V/D—Validator/Director

- **Primary DRIVE (Validator):** Motivated by respect, confidence, recognition, and personal value. They want to feel seen, strong, and capable.
- **Secondary DRIVE (Director):** Evaluates decisions based on personal freedom, independence, and opportunities to stand out boldly. They ask: *"Does this help me take control and stand out?"*
- **Sell to the Emotion:** Show how your offer highlights their strengths and validates who they are. Help them feel admired, respected, and empowered.
- **Close with Logic:** Position the solution as something they control that lets them chart their own path and step up with confidence.

V/R—Validator/Relator

- **Primary DRIVE (Validator):** Motivated by inner confidence and being appreciated for who they are.
- **Secondary DRIVE (Relator):** Considers decisions based on connection, influence, and the meaningful impact they can have

on others. They ask: *"Does this help me serve, connect, or be valued by others?"*

- **Sell to the Emotion:** Speak to their worth. Show how your offer helps them shine and gives them the confidence to fully show up.
- **Close with Logic:** Emphasize how this helps them build stronger relationships or make a meaningful impact in the lives of others.

V/I—Validator/Intellectual

- **Primary DRIVE (Validator):** Motivated by being respected, valued, and recognized.
- **Secondary DRIVE (Intellectual):** Evaluates decisions based on knowledge, understanding, and alignment with clear standards. They ask: *"Is this smart, solid, and grounded?"*
- **Sell to the Emotion:** Let them feel admired and competent. Show how your offer reinforces their unique strengths and helps them stand out.
- **Close with Logic:** Back it up with structure. Show that it's not just hype—it's thoughtful, tested, and designed to help them grow stronger.

V/E—Validator/Executive

- **Primary DRIVE (Validator):** Motivated by personal recognition and self-worth.
- **Secondary DRIVE (Executive):** Judges decisions based on effectiveness, performance, and achieving clear goals. They ask: *"Does this make me more effective and respected?"*
- **Sell to the Emotion:** Help them feel like the best version of themselves—powerful, respected, and worthy of admiration.

- **Close with Logic:** Show them how this solution makes them sharper, more productive, and more in control—someone others look up to and depend on.

E/D—Executive/Director

- **Primary DRIVE (Executive):** Motivated by achievement, results, and being in control. They want to win and make things happen.
- **Secondary DRIVE (Director):** Evaluates decisions based on opportunities for freedom, creativity, and independent leadership. They ask: *"Does this let me lead on my terms?"*
- **Sell to the Emotion:** Paint the win. Show how your solution helps them dominate their space, smash their goals, and stay in control of outcomes.
- **Close with Logic:** Position it as a powerful tool they can wield their own way—fast, bold, efficient, and with maximum impact.

E/R—Executive/Relator

- **Primary DRIVE (Executive):** Motivated by accomplishment and structured success. They want to deliver results and lead with excellence.
- **Secondary DRIVE (Relator):** Judges decisions based on their effect on relationships, influence, and meaningful outcomes for others. They ask: *"How does this help my team, family, or community?"*
- **Sell to the Emotion:** Focus on the outcome. Show them how your solution makes them look like the reliable leader who gets things done.

- **Close with Logic:** Emphasize how this also uplifts the people around them—how it drives team results or creates a ripple effect they can be proud of.

E/I—Executive/Intellectual

- **Primary DRIVE (Executive):** Motivated by control, winning, and high performance.
- **Secondary DRIVE (Intellectual):** Evaluates decisions based on efficiency, clear strategies, and logical design. They ask: *"Is this efficient, logical, and well-designed?"*
- **Sell to the Emotion:** Show how this will help them achieve more, faster—with less risk and more control. Let them feel like they're leveling up.
- **Close with Logic:** Back it up with clear reasoning, structure, and proven systems. They need to see the roadmap and how every part aligns with results.

E/V—Executive/Validator

- **Primary DRIVE (Executive):** Motivated by performance, productivity, and tangible wins.
- **Secondary DRIVE (Validator):** Judges decisions based on recognition, personal value, and alignment with their identity. They ask: *"Will this elevate how others see me?"*
- **Sell to the Emotion:** Let them feel like a winner. Show how this move earns them respect, status, and credibility.
- **Close with Logic:** Point out how this solution positions them to be recognized for their excellence—by their peers, their team, or the industry.

You've just seen how to sell to all 20 DRIVE combinations. Now let's put it to the test. One company had all the advantages, market share, history, and access. But they blew it, because they didn't speak to the buyer's DRIVE. And the competitor who did? They walked away with a billion-dollar brand. This is the story of Steph Curry, and how one pitch changed everything.

By 2013, Steph Curry was on the verge of a breakout . . . and on the edge of being overlooked. Coming out of Davidson College, he wasn't the typical NBA prospect. He wasn't the tallest. He wasn't the fastest. But he had a few other things: relentless work ethic, deadly accuracy, and a belief that he could prove everyone wrong. Curry wasn't just playing to win—he was playing to be seen. And not just as a player, but as someone whose presence truly mattered.

As a Validator/Executive, he wanted to be recognized not just for his stats, but for his story. That's the Validator in him. The Executive in him wanted results, a clear path forward, and a company that saw the same vision he did. He didn't want flash. He wanted focus. He didn't want to be part of someone else's brand story—he wanted to build his own.

When his Nike contract was up for renewal in 2013, everything should have been a slam dunk. Nike held 95.5% of the basketball sneaker market. His godfather worked for the company. He wore Nike in college. He was already on their roster. By all accounts, Curry was a lock.

But what happened next is a masterclass in misunderstanding someone's DRIVE.

The meeting took place in a generic conference room on the second floor of the Oakland Marriott, just three levels below the Golden State Warriors' practice facility. No branding. No energy. No show of force. Famed Nike executive Lynn Merritt—LeBron's right hand and a key power broker—wasn't there. That absence didn't just feel like a scheduling oversight. It felt personal. To a Validator/Executive like Curry, the message was loud and clear: he was not a priority.

During the presentation, the missteps piled up. A Nike rep mis-pronounced his name as "Steph-on," and a slide from the deck still had Kevin Durant's name on it. It was a recycled pitch. A copy-and-paste job. Nike wasn't seeing him. They weren't pitching to him. They were treating him like just another player. For a Validator, that's the ultimate disconnect. And for a Validator/Exec-utive, it's a deal-breaker. No recognition. No clarity. No vision for what they could build together.

Then came Under Armour.

They didn't have the market share. They didn't have the prestige. But they saw Curry and what he could be.

Under Armour built a campaign around his story. They invited his input. Let him lead and made him the face of their future. They didn't just offer a contract—they offered belonging. Recognition. Legacy. And they gave him the keys to help shape it.

That one decision—to go where his DRIVE felt understood—reshaped two companies.

Under Armour's basketball line exploded. The Curry One became a bestseller. His signature shoe line helped generate $14 billion in growth. In 2023, they doubled down and signed Curry to a lifetime contract—elevating him to President of Curry Brand, giving him control of product direction, social impact campaigns, and more.

And then, on the court? He made history.

In 2025, Steph Curry became the first player in NBA history to hit 4,000 three-pointers. No one else is even close. As of that milestone, the next active player—James Harden—is nearly 900 threes behind. Steph didn't just rewrite the record books—he created a category of his own.

All of that came from one pivotal moment. One pitch.

Nike had the advantage: 95.5% of the market. His godfather on staff. Years of history. But they misread the room and definitely misread the man. They treated him like another athlete on the roster. Under Armour treated him like a legend in the making.

This was the same player with the same talent. The difference was two pitches. Nike had the competitive edge. Under Armour had the personal insight. And in the end, the sale went to the brand that sold to Curry's DRIVE.

This isn't just a sales system—it's a shift in how you see people. You now have the tools to connect at the deepest level, speak the language that resonates, and close in a way that aligns with who your customer truly is. When you Sell to the Primary and Close to the Secondary, you don't just win deals—you build trust, loyalty, and influence that lasts.

Now it's your turn. Go speak their DRIVE. Go make your impact. And go become the salesperson they'll never forget.

The DRIVE Sales System

S.—Start with Their D.R.I.V.E.
A.—Assess Their Needs
L.—Leverage Your Solutions
E.—Eliminate Their Concerns
S.—Sell Them Their D.R.I.V.E. Solution

12

Fortune is in the Follow Up

In 2009, Ryan Serhant was a struggling actor turned rookie real estate agent in New York City. With no listings, no clients, and no reputation, he spent his days hustling—often in coffee shops, striking up conversations with strangers who looked like they might be in the market for a home. One day, while sitting in a Starbucks on 49th and Madison, he met a woman who, along with her husband, was casually browsing for properties with a budget of around $1 million. They chatted, exchanged information, spoke back and forth for six months—and then . . . nothing.

But Ryan (E/D) didn't let the lead die. Every other week, for eight years, he sent them listings—always relevant, always timely, always professional. No replies. No signs of life. Just silence.

Then, out of the blue, the husband finally wrote back. "I've been busy," he said. "But I've been getting your emails. Let's talk." Despite knowing other agents and brokers, the man appreciated Ryan's persistence and decided to give him a shot. By this time, the husband and wife had divorced. Ryan ended up selling the man a $40 million home in the Hamptons—and the ex-wife a $16 million property—earning a seven-figure commission in the process.

Reflecting on this experience, Ryan often says, "My ability to follow up with you until you die is the entire way that I sell properties."

If you want to be phenomenal at sales, live by this motto: Follow Up Till They Buy or Die.

Where 94% of Sales Die

These are the hard facts that should be posted on every wall of every sales office in the world.

According to Dr. Herbert True, a marketing specialist at Notre Dame:

- 44% of salespeople make one contact . . . and stop.
- 24% make a second contact . . . and stop.
- 14% make a third contact . . . and stop.
- 12% make a fourth contact . . . and stop.

That means 94% of salespeople give up by the fourth attempt.

Now, look at what Dr. True discovered with regards to when the actual sales happen:

- 2% of sales happen on the 1st contact.
- 3% happen on the 2nd.
- 5% on the 3rd.
- 10% on the 4th.
- 80% of all sales happen after the 5th contact.

Let that sink in. Ninety-four percent of salespeople quit right before the money shows up. They walk away just as the relationship is starting to warm up. They vanish before the real objection surfaces, before trust is built, before belief kicks in, before clarity is given. They leave the deal—and the commission—behind.

Meanwhile, the top six percent? They stay in the game, even if, like Ryan, it takes years. Then, they get paid. These people aren't better or smarter. They simply don't stop. They follow up

with intention, precision, and consistency. Because they understand this truth: *the fortune is in the follow-up.*

Many salespeople are great at lead generation but terrible at follow-up. And because of this, they're constantly forced to find new leads. It becomes a never-ending cycle of starting over—always chasing, never closing. I've sat in sales training meetings where the trainer proudly declared, "If they don't buy, let 'em die. Move on and get new prospects." But that's not how elite salespeople think. A "no" today isn't a "no" forever—it usually means *not now.* There's a fine line between being persistent and being a pest, and that line is drawn by the value you create with every interaction.

In the early 1980s, a renowned college basketball coach was conducting a clinic at a U.S. Army base in West Germany. After his session, a towering young man approached him, seeking guidance on improving his basketball skills. The coach, taken aback by the youth's stature, inquired, "How long have you been in the Army, soldier?" The young man replied, "I'm not in the Army, sir. I'm thirteen years old."

Impressed by the teenager's presence and determination, the coach saw potential where others might not. Recognizing that the boy lacked refined skills but possessed an undeniable drive to learn and improve, the coach committed to mentoring him. Over the next several years, he sent weekly letters filled with training tips, motivational quotes, and personal encouragement. This consistent outreach wasn't about recruiting; it was about nurturing a young man's growth in the sport of his choice.

As the teenager matured, his basketball prowess blossomed. By his junior year in high school, he had become a sought-after talent, with numerous colleges vying for his commitment. Despite the flurry of attention, he chose to play for the coach who had believed in him from the beginning—the one who had invested time and effort without any immediate return.

That young man was Shaquille O'Neal (D/R). The coach was Dale Brown (R/V) of LSU. Their story is a testament to the power of persistent follow-up and genuine, selfless mentorship. Coach Brown's unwavering commitment didn't just secure a top recruit; it forged a lifelong bond and played a pivotal role in shaping one of basketball's greatest legends.

Why Most Salespeople Don't Follow Up

So why do 94% of salespeople stop following up after the fourth contact? It's not because they're lazy. And it's not because they're afraid of hearing "no." Professionals hear "no" all the time, that's just part of the game. The real reason they stop is far deeper, and more personal. In the original *DRIVE Sales* book, we introduced the five DRIVE Principles. Principle #3 reveals the breakthrough: *"Subconsciously or consciously, you will do anything within your belief system to defend and support your DRIVE."* In other words, we don't follow up because we're trying to protect ourselves—not our ego, but our DRIVE. Each of us interprets rejection, silence, or hesitation through the lens of our deepest motivation. And when that objection feels like a threat to who we are, we avoid it, even if we don't realize we're doing it.

Check out these examples, distilled down to each particular DRIVE:

Directors may feel like a rejection threatens their freedom or their ability to overcome challenges. It disrupts their sense of independence and forward momentum, so they disengage.

Relators may interpret a "no" as personal disconnection, it feels like the relationship is strained or the bond is broken and they don't want to make it worse.

Intellectuals might see an objection as a failure of knowledge, a breakdown in understanding, and that can feel disorienting, so instead of following up, they retreat.

Validators often tie their identity to being respected and admired. If they sense they've lost credibility or aren't being taken seriously, they'd rather withdraw than risk further rejection.

Executives are wired to win. They may see a "no" as a personal defeat or an attack on their performance. To protect their track record, they move on rather than push through.

These are the unseen reasons most salespeople vanish after a few follow-ups. It's not the lead that's dead, it's their DRIVE that subconsciously feels threatened. And until a salesperson understands how their DRIVE responds to resistance, they'll keep pulling back, right when the fortune is finally within reach.

How to Reclaim Your Power

If fear is what stops you, then clarity is what gets you moving again. The key is to stop taking objections personally and start interpreting them through the lens of your customer—not your DRIVE.

This doesn't mean ignoring your DRIVE. It means knowing it so well that you can spot when it's running the show instead of collaborating with you for your success. When you can see the difference between *their resistance* and *your reaction*, you regain control.

Here's a simple rule:

When you feel hesitation, pause and ask—am I protecting my DRIVE or progressing the deal?

If you're protecting your DRIVE, you'll pull back. If you're progressing the deal, you'll lean in—with clarity, not fear.

And here's the turning point: the best way to protect your DRIVE is to learn how to *reframe objections without getting defensive.* That's what this next framework is all about.

How to Handle Objections: R.E.S.T.A.T.E.—The Elegant Objection Turnaround

R—Respect Their Concern

Don't dodge it or dismiss it. Respecting someone's concern shows you're listening and honoring their perspective without agreeing or backing down. It demonstrates confidence, patience, and emotional intelligence. This builds immediate rapport and lowers the emotional temperature of the conversation.

When a buyer says something like, *"I'm just not sure if this is the right time,"* respond with: *"I totally respect that—it's a big decision, and timing matters."*

That line disarms tension and validates a concern. You're not pushing. You're aligning. Respect shifts the conversation from resistance to trust.

Why This Works:

- Director—Honors their need for control. They stay open because they don't feel boxed in.
- Relator—Builds relational safety. They feel heard, not pressured.
- Intellectual—Shows thoughtfulness. They respect conversations that make space for nuance.
- Validator—Affirms their voice. They feel acknowledged, not challenged.
- Executive—Projects confidence and poise. They trust people who don't flinch under pressure.

E—Empathize with Their Position

Empathy enhances trust. Most objections are emotionally rooted, even when they sound logical. When you empathize, you signal,

"You're not crazy for feeling this." That calms the emotional brain, and when the emotion drops, logic can re-enter.

This is where you humanize the process. *"It's totally normal to pause here—most clients do when the decision really matters."* When you say something similar to this, the tension breaks. They realize they're not stuck—they're just human.

Why This Works:

- Director—It shows that you're not trying to trap them. You're respecting their space and independence, which ironically makes them more open to moving forward.
- Relator—It creates emotional safety. They need to know they're not alone.
- Intellectual—It provides a calm space for logic to reengage. Once emotion is acknowledged, they can reason again.
- Validator—It reassures them that they're not failing or being judged. They feel seen and respected.
- Executive—It models composure and control. They admire empathy that doesn't flinch under pressure.

S—Spot the DRIVE Behind It

Don't treat the surface-level objection—treat the core DRIVE that's hesitating. As a reminder, you sell to the Primary (Emotion) and close to the Secondary (Logic). Here is a sample of how this type of resistance may show up.

Examples of Emotional Resistance (Primary):

- "It just doesn't feel like the right move."
- "I'm not sure I'm ready."
- "I need to sit with it."

Examples of Logical Hesitation (Secondary):

- "What's the next step again?"
- "Can I see a breakdown of deliverables?"
- "I'm not sure how we'd fund this."

Spot the true DRIVE behind the objection and meet it directly. Reassure the DRIVE, not just the doubt.

- **Director:** "Is this going to limit my freedom?"
- **Relator:** "Will this create tension with my team or family?"
- **Intellectual:** "Is there enough logic or proof?"
- **Validator:** "Will I look smart—or be seen as foolish?"
- **Executive:** "Is this going to help me win—or put me at risk?"

T—Tell a Story

We've all heard it: *Facts tell—stories sell.* One reason why? Stories bypass resistance. They create safety. Instead of pushing facts or telling someone what to do, you're saying, *"Here's what someone like you did . . ."* This approach disarms the need to defend and opens the door to self-reflection. It's one of the most elegant ways to shift perspective without confrontation.

Your story should mirror their concern, then resolve it. Keep it short—aim for sixty to ninety seconds or less. Follow this structure:

Situation ➡ Objection ➡ Action ➡ Outcome

Example: *"One client had the same hesitation—she was worried it'd slow her down. But she said yes to the audit, and two weeks later, she landed her biggest deal."*

Let the story do the convincing. It's less pressure and more persuasion.

Why This Works:

- Director—They picture themselves as the hero of the story. It appeals to their desire for bold outcomes.
- Relator—Connects through a shared experience. It reassures them they're not alone.
- Intellectual—Provides a real-world example they can logically analyze.
- Validator—Helps them imagine future recognition by seeing someone else succeed.
- Executive—Showcases a win. That's their language—results, not theory.

A—Ask a Clarifying Question

Questions are the scalpel of sales. A good one cuts straight to clarity without triggering defense. Your goal here isn't to battle the objection—it's to *invite their own insight*. This step reactivates logic, especially for Intellectuals and Executives who need to *think* their way to conviction.

Use questions that flip the frame and lower resistance.

- *"If timing weren't the issue, would this be the right fit?"*
- *"If we could solve that part, what else would be holding you back?"*

These questions don't trap—they free. They shift the buyer from defending hesitation to discovering opportunity. Most objections dissolve under their own weight when examined with the right question.

Why This Works:

- Director—Gives them a sense of freedom. The decision feels like theirs.

- Relator—Opens the door gently. They feel invited, not pressured.
- Intellectual—Triggers reflection and analysis—right in their zone.
- Validator—Makes them feel smart for uncovering their own insight.
- Executive—Fast-tracks the win. They move when the path is clear.

T—Tie it Back to Their DRIVE

Now that the objection is softened, it's time to reconnect them to why they were here in the first place. This isn't about pitching harder—it's about re-selling the *vision* through their language, their values, and their DRIVE. Speak to their Primary DRIVE to reignite emotional conviction.

You don't need to convince; you need to remind. Tie the next step directly to the motivator they shared before fear crept in.

- Director—"This step gives you more freedom, not more complexity."
- Relator—"This brings the people around you into alignment."
- Intellectual—"This is the cleanest, smartest next move based on everything you shared."
- Validator—"This puts you in a position to shine."
- Executive—"This locks in results. This is how you win."

You're not closing them yet—they're returning to their own *why*. And that's what makes the decision feel right.

Why This Works:

- Director—Reaffirms freedom and purpose, not pressure.
- Relator—Aligns the decision with relationships and shared success.

- Intellectual—Anchors the choice in logic and alignment.
- Validator—Makes them feel recognized and powerful.
- Executive—Confirms results, control, and momentum.

E—Earn the Micro-Yes

No pressure. No cliff jumps. At this point, you can initiate a confident nudge toward progress. Big commitments feel risky when objections are fresh—but micro-yeses build momentum. That's how top salespeople keep deals alive without chasing or pushing.

The goal here isn't the close—it's movement. Schedule the next call. Ask for feedback. Offer a trial run or quick walkthrough. Keep the decision small, simple, and friction-free.

Examples:

- *"Want me to sketch out what implementation would look like so we can see the gaps?"*
- *"How about a short call next week to review options together?"*
- *"Let me send over a one-pager—if it resonates, we'll keep going."*

Micro-yeses are low-risk for them, but high-leverage for you. Stack enough of them, and the sale closes itself.

Why This Works:

- Director—Honors their freedom of choice and gives them a creative path forward.
- Relator—Feels like a collaboration, not a commitment trap.
- Intellectual—Reduces ambiguity and builds logical next steps.
- Validator—Makes them feel smart for progressing without pressure.
- Executive—Feels efficient and strategic, just the way they like it.

Why Small Yeses Lead to Big Wins

If you've ever wondered why follow-up works, here's the psychology behind it.

In his book *Influence: Science and Practice*, Dr. Robert Cialdini shares a fascinating study by psychologists Jonathan Freedman and Scott Fraser. They went door-to-door in a California neighborhood and asked homeowners if they would be willing to install a huge, unsightly billboard in their front yard that read, "Drive Carefully." The result? Only 17% agreed.

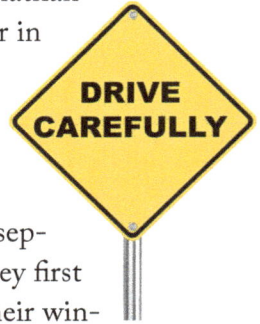

But then they tried something different. With a separate group of homeowners, they started smaller. They first asked if they could place a tiny three-inch sign in their window that said, "Be a Safe Driver." Most people said yes—it was easy, noninvasive, and aligned with their values.

Two weeks later, the researchers returned and asked the same homeowners if they would now be willing to install the massive front-yard billboard.

This time, 76% said yes.

That's a 450% increase, just because they had already said yes to something small.

This is the power of follow-up done right. It's not about pushing. It's about stacking value and permission over time. Small commitments build comfort. Comfort builds trust. And trust opens the door for the bigger yes.

In sales, your small touchpoints—your check-ins, updates, insights, or encouragement—are the three-inch signs. When delivered with care, consistency, and value, they warm the relationship and pave the way for bigger commitments. Follow-up isn't about wearing someone down. It's about warming them up. Remember Ryan's story? It doesn't have to take years, but this warming process is key to incredible turn-arounds.

So how do you follow up in a way that builds trust, earns micro-yeses, and avoids coming across as a pest? You need a framework—a rhythm you can repeat with confidence. That's where F.O.L.L.O.W.™ comes in.

F.O.L.L.O.W.™—The Follow-Up That Closes

Follow-up isn't nagging. It's leadership. When done right, it builds trust, maintains momentum, and turns hesitation into clarity. The best follow-up doesn't feel like chasing—it feels like serving. Here's how to do it the right way, using the F.O.L.L.O.W.™ method:

F—Frame the Follow-Up

Don't leave your next step to chance. Before the conversation ends, set a clear expectation of when, how, and why you'll follow up. It builds professionalism, eliminates ghosting, and positions you as a leader in the relationship.

Be proactive: *"I would love to reconnect Thursday at 10am so I can share those numbers you asked for. Does Thursday work, or do you have a different time that fits your schedule better?"* When you frame the next step before the call ends, you're not hoping for a callback—you're locking in a runway.

Why This Works:

- **Director**—Respects their time and autonomy—no surprises.
- **Relator**—Feels relational and considerate, not transactional.
- **Intellectual**—Appreciates structure and forethought.
- **Validator**—Shows professionalism and follow-through.
- **Executive**—Demonstrates control and efficiency.

O—Offer Value Again

Every touchpoint should bring something new to the table. Insight. Perspective. A tool. A quick story. If you want to stay relevant, you have to stay valuable.

Don't follow up merely to "check in." Instead, try this: *Just sent over a checklist our top clients use—I thought of you when we discussed simplifying your process.*" When your follow-up delivers value, you're not chasing—you're serving.

Why This Works:

- Director—Keeps things fresh, forward-moving, and relevant to their journey.
- Relator—Shows you're thinking about them as a person, not a prospect.
- Intellectual—Gives them something to analyze, weigh, or implement.
- Validator—Makes them feel important, seen, and remembered.
- Executive—Reinforces ROI and practical usefulness.

L—Listen for Change

Circumstances shift. Goals evolve. Emotions fluctuate. Don't assume yesterday's priorities still apply today. Great follow-up includes listening for what's changed and adapting with it.

Ask open, low-pressure questions: *"Since we last spoke, has anything shifted in your priorities or timeline?"* Stay curious. Follow-up isn't a script—it's a temperature check.

Why This Works:

- Director—Respects their freedom to pivot or explore new angles.

- Relator—Invites a deeper, more personal conversation.
- Intellectual—Engages their love of thoughtful dialogue.
- Validator—Makes them feel heard and relevant to the process.
- Executive—Shows that you're agile and results-focused.

L—Leverage Their DRIVE

Generic follow-up falls flat. When you speak directly to their DRIVE, your message hits the emotional target—and that's what makes it land.

Tailor your message:

- Director: "This next step gives you more freedom and momentum."
- Relator: "This will bring the people around you into alignment."
- Intellectual: "This is the most strategic, thought-through path."
- Validator: "This really highlights what makes you stand out."
- Executive: "This locks in a competitive edge and keeps you ahead."

Personalized language creates emotional traction. You're not following up—you're reinforcing their *why*.

Why This Works:

- Director—Reinforces independence and impact.
- Relator—Speaks to purpose and connection.
- Intellectual—Matches their need for precision and thoughtfulness.
- Validator—Builds identity and confidence.
- Executive—Aligns with progress, performance, and results.

O—Overcome Resistance

Don't avoid objections—anticipate them. In your follow-up, revisit the core hesitation and gently reframe it. When you show that you understand the objection and can still move forward, you remove pressure and restore clarity.

Try something like: *"You mentioned time was a concern. If this actually saves you 5+ hours a week, would it be worth revisiting?"* You're not pushing—you're rebalancing the scale.

Why This Works:

- Director—Feels like overcoming a challenge, not a trap.
- Relator—Appreciates the low-pressure invitation.
- Intellectual—Responds well to a rational reframing.
- Validator—Respects that their concerns were heard and addressed.
- Executive—Loves when the path to ROI becomes clearer.

W—Win the Micro-Yes

The fortune isn't just in the follow-up—it's in the next small step. Don't swing for the close. Instead, offer a micro-yes that keeps the door open and the decision moving.

Make the next step feel easy and logical:

- *"Do you feel like it makes sense to schedule a 15 minute alignment call?"*
- *"Would you like to have a side by side comparison so you can see the clear difference we have discussed?"*
- *"I'll send over a summary – if it offers everything you're looking for – what do you believe the next step should be?"*

Small commitments create movement. And movement closes deals.

Why This Works:

- Director—Respects their freedom to say yes without pressure.
- Relator—Feels low-stakes and relationship-driven.
- Intellectual—Keeps the process logical and clean.
- Validator—Lets them feel smart for progressing at their pace.
- Executive—Builds toward a close without wasting time.

As you master both the R.E.S.T.A.T.E. and F.O.L.L.O.W. frameworks, remember: every follow-up must be personalized to their DRIVE. One-size-fits-all doesn't work in high-stakes sales. Reflect on the opening story from the previous chapter—where I lost a multiple six-figure contract—because I failed to recognize that what resonates with one DRIVE can completely miss with another. Every touchpoint matters. Every message should be intentional, tailored, and crafted for maximum impact.

You Get 100% of What You Don't Ask For

My phone rang. "Hi, this is Stephanie. Who are you and why do I have flowers on my desk?"

"Thank you for calling me," I replied. "We are going to change the world with this movie, and I need your help to make it happen."

When I was filming my first movie (i-ology), I needed over 250 clips of High Definition (HD) stock footage. The average price per clip at the time was about $900. After researching the best company in the industry, I called the secretary and asked for the person in charge of stock footage. Upon getting her name, I called 1-800-FLOWERS and sent her a basket of flowers with a note that said,

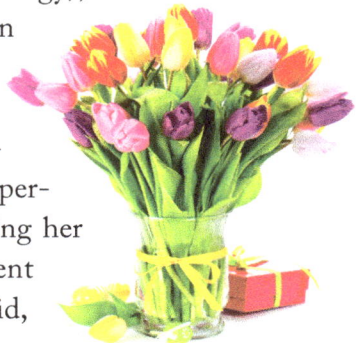

"Thank you in advance for helping me with my movie project. Sincerely, Woody (XXX) XXX-XXXX."

I received that phone call within three days from Stephanie. I went on to tell her how I needed her company to donate stock footage for my movie that was going to change the world. Firmly, she replied, "No, we are a business. We sell stock footage for a living." She instructed me it was impossible; the company would not donate the required footage. I tried every *ASK. Don't Tell* technique I could think of.

After about fifteen minutes of getting told "no," she finally said, "If you will send me your script, distribution plan, shooting dates, and locations, I will take it to my boss. Call us back in thirty days and we can discuss it."

"I will have it all to you in forty-eight hours," I replied. In those moments, I actually didn't have anything she asked for, so it was a very long forty-eight hours trying to make it all up. At day fifteen, I sent both Stephanie and her boss movie passes, a box of popcorn with candies, and a note saying, "Enjoy a movie on me." On day twenty-nine, I sent a box of chocolates and another note saying, "Thank you in advance for helping make my movie."

When the time arrived for our conference call, both Stephanie and her boss were grateful for the gifts but said, "Woody, as you know, we are a business and we cannot give you the number of clips you want for free. What we are willing to do is sell you as many clips as you need for $50 apiece. Would that work?"

I had spent roughly $257.83 on their gifts and now I was saving over $200,000 for stock footage. I was sure they could hear me smiling when I said, "Would you like a credit card or wire transfer?"

Why did such a crazy approach work? Dr. David Schwartz said, "Man's most compelling non-biological hunger is to feel important." When we make others feel important, it changes the way we do business and that is the point of the DRIVE Sales System.

Conclusion: This Is Just the Beginning

Thank you for taking this journey with us.

If you've made it this far, you're not just a reader—you're a rare breed. You're someone who's committed to mastering not only the *mechanics* of sales, but the *psychology* behind why people say yes. You've invested time, energy, and focus to understand yourself, your clients, and how to speak the five languages of DRIVE.

Between us, Bob and I have over seventy-five years of frontline sales experience—across industries, markets, economies, and eras. There's no way to download all of that into a single 200-page book. But this isn't the end. This is your launch pad.

We created this system not to impress but to equip. And now that you've got the foundation, the next level comes through conversation, coaching, and real-world application. That's what our weekly mastermind is all about.

Join us at **DriveSalesMastermind.com.** Ask questions. Share your wins. Get insight tailored to your exact challenges. Surround yourself with high performers who speak your language and stretch your standards. Sales is too big a game to play alone—and you weren't meant to.

We can't wait to hear your success stories.

"Invest In Yourself—It's Your Greatest Asset." —Warren Buffett

Imagine an investment that multiplies your sales reach by 400% and transforms your closing ratios. Imagine a future where you no longer lose 80% of your potential sales because you fully understand what DRIVES your customers. A future where your sales targets are not just met, but consistently exceeded. That future starts today.

Here's what awaits you:

- **Unlock Your Potential with a Free Consultation:** Let's connect one-on-one in a personalized session to explore how the DRIVE Sales System can revolutionize your approach and dramatically increase your sales reach.

- **Amplify Your Sales by 400%:** Master the 20/80 Rule. Exceed your quotas by learning the precise language that resonates with your buyers, turning potential leads into loyal customers.

- **Always Be Closing with DRIVE+AI:** Access your custom DRIVE+AI assistant—available 24/7—to navigate through any sales challenge. From enhancing your social media presence to optimizing your marketing strategies, ensure you're always a step ahead.

- **Join the Exclusive DRIVE Sales Mastermind Community:** Gain access to our private members-only network, weekly live mastermind calls, and a vault of over 100 high-impact training videos. Surround yourself with top performers who speak your language, challenge your thinking, and elevate your game every single week.

For Sales Managers, Trainers, CEOs, Recruiters, and Solo Sales Professionals: Whether you lead a team or carry the quota yourself, we understand the pressure to perform and the challenge of staying motivated. If you're ready to build a culture of clarity, consistency, and connection—or just want a proven system to help you sell smarter—let's talk. Together, we can equip you (and your team) to thrive in today's competitive market.

Step into a new era of sales excellence. Visit **DriveSalesMastermind.com** to book your free consultation (valued at $250) and to join our weekly mastermind. You don't have to do this alone. Let's journey towards transformative results together!

www.ingramcontent.com/pod-product-compliance
Lightning Source LLC
Chambersburg PA
CBHW041918190326
41458CB00055B/6937/J